CUBA: 50 YEARS OF PLAYING AMERICAN FOOTBALL

Christopher A. Perez

Published in the United States 2016

ISBN: 978-1533551818

"These boys [Cuban football players] are green but good. They block fairly well and tackle like they like it. And when it comes to running, well . . ."

University of Havana Coach Robert Zuppke

CONTENTS

PREFACE

I decided to write this book because I'm a HUGE football fan and wanted other fans to know about Cuba's seldom known history of playing American football, in specifically, college football. Watching football all my life, I had no idea that the sport was actually played in the small island nation until I came across an old photo in the University of Miami's Digital Archives collection. The photo was dated November 25, 1926 and it featured a football game that was dubbed the "Thanksgiving Classic" between the newly-established University of Miami program and the University of Havana football team. Having sparked my interest, I began researching more about the subject. The research revealed that Cuba had a short but extensive history in American football that began in the beginning of the 20th century and last for nearly 50 years.

Being a first generation Cuban American and having heard many stories of the "old country" from relatives, I was now the one telling the story of how American football made its way to Cuba. This subject is especially fascinating and close to heart as it combines my fathers' homeland with a sport that I passionately love. Ultimately, football was abruptly abolished after a new oppressive government regime took power in the late 1950s. Coincidingly, it was around the time when my family fled the island and migrated to the United States in search of freedom. I hope that you enjoy this book and it will give you a deeper insight into the sport of football as it relates to the way Cuba impacted the sport.

INTRODUCTION

When you think of Cuba you normally picture hand rolled cigars, Cuban food, and conga music. Perhaps Ricky Ricardo from the popular *I Love Lucy* television show comes to mind. One of the last things probably has to be American football. You may ask yourself, "What does Cuba have anything to do with football?" Sure, the country is better known for their love of their national sport *béisbol* (baseball) and amateur boxing but unbeknownst to most people is Cuba's history of playing football. In fact, Cuba fielded a college football team, the University of Havana (UH) Caribes, before 40 current teams in the National Collegiate Athletic Association (NCAA) Division I Football Bowl Subdivision (FBS). That would currently place the Caribes program 89th amongst the 128 active FBS college football programs by year established (UH was not officially recognized as part of the NCAA). A quick side note, *Caribes* is Spanish for "Caribs". The University of Havana chose the moniker to honor the Caribs who were the indigenous people that inhabited the Lesser Antilles and whom the Caribbean Sea was named after.

CREATING SOMETHING SPECIAL

From 1906-1956, there were over 50 games that were either played by a Cuban football team against an American opponent or where Cuba hosted an international college football game. While the University of Havana played the majority of those games, the school wasn't the only Cuban institution that fielded a football team. Athletic social clubs, a police sports club, and several branches of the Cuban military each established football teams that competed with America universities. Some of these games were played before a college football rule governing body was established which gave the teams autonomy on who they would they would like to play. Even after the Intercollegiate Athletic Association of the United States (IAAUS) was established there weren't rules that addressed this issue. As a result, American college football teams sometimes played club football teams that weren't even associated with a university while others played foreign universities, usually Canadian schools. During this time college football was still in its infancy and the IAAUS, who would be later renamed the National Collegiate Athletic Association (NCAA), focused more on making new rules to make the sport safer to play and not so much on the opponents that teams should schedule.

Cuba's close proximity to the Unites States made it attractive for college teams within the two neighboring countries to play. The 90 miles that separates the U.S. and Cuba was often a shorter distance for an American college team to travel then it would be to play an opponent in another state. Furthermore, the United States and Cuba had developed longstanding diplomatic ties and Cubans often associated more with their neighbors to the north than their Caribbean neighbors. This is evident in the sports that Cubans chose to play. Cubans played sports that are popular in North America and participate less in sports that are more prevalent in the Caribbean such as soccer and cricket. American football seemed like the next logical athletic endeavor that the Cubans would like to try their hands at after trying baseball and basketball.

Ever since a Cuban football team played it first football game there was a struggle to create lasting interest in the sport. The University of Havana football team and club teams would schedule games with American opponents on a biannual basis, sometimes longer. By 1920, football in Cuba began to gain traction as it became a larger presence in the societal sports community. Also, the football games in island slowly evolved from being solely a participatory sport to becoming a spectator driven event. Now fans were attending games more than ever. With heightened excitement, American and Cuban teams began to play one another consistently on an annual basis and rivalries began to naturally develop.

THE END OF THE GAME

The aftermath of the Cuban Revolution in the mid- to late 1950s marked the end of football in Cuba. Fidel Castro and his allies were able to overthrow then U.S.-backed Cuban President Fulgencio Batista to create a new socialist state. After taking office, Fidel Castro famously proclaimed, "If there ever was in the history of humanity an enemy who was truly universal, an enemy whose acts and moves trouble the entire world, threaten the entire world, attack the entire world in any way or another, that real and really universal enemy is precisely Yankee imperialism" (Brewer). Castro believed that Cuba had become too Americanized and wanted the country to distance themselves from the United States in every aspect. As part of his cultural cleansing of Cuban society, Castro abolished American football from ever being played again.

During the relatively short time that football was played in island, Cuban football teams played over 20 different opponents. The majority of the teams were comprised of universities from the South. Five of their opponents would eventually go on to win a NCAA Division I Championship and they include: Louisiana State University (LSU), University of Alabama, University of Florida, University of Miami, and the University of Mississippi (Ole Miss). Cuban football teams also notably played against eventual NCAA Division II champions in Georgia Southern University and the Mississippi Southern College (University of Southern Mississippi). That is a pretty astonishing feat for a country that would go on to eliminate the sport entirely. Today, the country's participation in American college football is essentially part of its forgotten pre-revolutionary past. Evidence of football ever being played is nearly non-existent in Cuba. The *Federación Cubana de Atletismo* (Cuban Athletics Federation), the organization that maintains the country's athletics records, does not contain any traces of Cuba's participation in football.

POSSIBLE REVIVAL?

Following the Cuban Revolution, the U.S. would go on to sever all ties with the communist nation. For a half-century, the two countries remained bitter enemies but in December 2014 there was a shocking new development. U.S. President Barack Obama announced that the United States will restore full diplomatic relations with its longtime Cold War foe. Shortly thereafter, Obama visited Cuba and attended a goodwill exhibition baseball game with Cuban President Raúl Castro (Fidel's younger brother). The game featured the Tampa Bay Rays versus the Cuban National team in the capital city of Havana. With America slowly reestablishing relations with Cuba, will football make its way back on the island? No one knows for certain but subtle signs seem to point that that they will. In October 2015, it has been rumored that the National Football League (NFL) was considering hosting a future game in Cuba. The NFL, which has tried to expand their brand internationally, has never played a game in the Caribbean country. NFL executives would love to add 11 million more fans to their ever popular league. In March 2016, LSU football head coach Les Miles made national headlines when he visited the island. Other universities have traveled to Cuba to compete against Cuban universities in baseball and basketball. Hopefully the normalization will lead to Cuba playing *fútbol Americano* once again. The Cubans will have to essentially relearn the game but it's not an impossible task. Time will only tell.

CUBA

THE LOVELIEST LAND THAT HUMAN EYES HAVE EVER SEEN

Come to Cuba

CHAPTER ONE

Unassuming Origins

American football's origins in Cuba was due to two main events that took place within a relatively close period of time. Each entity will be discussed in their entirety but first we have to examine the condition of athletics in the island in order to get a true understanding of how American football made its way to the Cuba.

SEGREGATED SPORTS

Before the revolution, the U.S. and Cuban governments enjoyed a working relationship and citizens of both countries were free to travel back and forth with relative ease. Well-to-do Cuban families often sent their children to the States to study abroad at American universities. The students participated in various sports at school including American football and they would bring their newfound knowledge of the game back home. "Clubs centering around North American sports proliferated across the island" (Pérez). The private social clubs purchased the majority of the country's sports fields and athletic facilities. Membership to the clubs were limited to the wealthy class. The rest of the Cuban population were automatically denied access to the clubs and, more importantly, their athletic fields. These social clubs also rejected applicants based on race.

Blacks, *mulatos* (mixed races), and Jews were denied membership. Even President Batista, who was multi-racial, was denied membership to the exclusive Havana Yacht Club. Batista became an "honorary" member of the less stringent Havana Country Club. Even with his special membership status, Batista's skin color still prevented him from entering the clubhouse through the main entrance. The Havana Biltmore Yacht and Country Club, as it was later renamed, made him enter through a separate entrance on the side of the building so that he wouldn't be seen entering through the front of the clubhouse.

THE ARISTOCRATS

Vedado Tennis Club (VTC) was established on June 9, 1902 "by Cubans who has taken up tennis during previous residence in the United States" (Pérez). Located in the most modern section of the capital, the Vedado social club was strictly for Havana's ultra-elite. Cuban Presidents Mario García Menocal and Gerardo Machado were members as were Orestes Ferrara, the Cuban Ambassador to the United States, and Cuban Olympic Committee President Porfirio Franca. While the club's name may invoke the notion that it solely centered around tennis, Vedado was more of a recreational social club that happened to play sports. The VTC hosted balls, banquets, galas, and theatrical performances that Jay Gatsby certainly would have approved of. The clubhouse itself was a Spanish Renaissance style three-story building that had identical towers on each end. For 3 pesos a month (approximately $100 today) members enjoyed the endless amenities that the Vedado Tennis Club had to offer.

As far as sports were concerned, the club participated in fencing, soccer, rowing, baseball, and eventually American football. The VTC had a fairly limited overall impact of football in Cuba but they did manage to play two important games against American opponents. The Vedado Marquises hosted the University of Florida in 1912 and played the University of Miami in 1928 in Coral Gables, Florida. In August 1909, a different social club called the *Club Atlético de Cuba* (CAC), which translates to Cuban Athletic Club, was established. Unlike the Vedado Club, the CAC originated from humbler beginnings. The idea for the club took place at a Havana Young Men's Christian Association (YMCA) that served both American and Cuban boys. Some of the boys that lived at the YMCA banded together and became the founder members of the Cuban Athletic Club.

The CAC clubhouse was located in Paseo del Prado, a scenic promenade that divided Central Havana and historic Old Havana. The athletic club's activities only revolved around sports. They participated in baseball, basketball, boxing, soccer, tennis, rowing, and American football. The club's teams were nicknamed the Orangemen or the *Tigres* (Tigers) depending on the year that the team played. Club members included Vice Secretary-General Lorenzo Tur and Cuban Olympic Committee President Miguel Angel Moenck.

Vedado Tennis Club, Havana, early 1900s.

The men who played football for the Cuban club teams were unlike the football players in the U.S. These men were influential members of society that were more known for their skills as writers, painters, intellectuals, and sons of dignitaries instead of their football prowess. CAC members like Cuban writer Pablo de la Torriente Brau (pictured right) would come together in the winter to practice for the upcoming football season. The CAC football team dressed in the club uniform that consisted of a black sweater with an orange stripe and epaulettes on the shoulders. Not typical of the usual football uniform, the garments were meant to show off the club's status, power, and wealth.

After the football season the men returned to their regular professions. For Vedado Tennis Club and Cuban Athletic Club football players, competing in the sport was more of an accomplishment that one fulfilled to later boast about with other influential club members. It was definitely not something that these men wanted to pursue professionally. Nevertheless, the CAC's sports-only mentality made them the more dominant of the two clubs.

THE SERVICEMEN

Following Cuba's independence from Spain in the late 19th century, the U.S. military had a consistent naval presence on the island. During periods of downtime, sailors often played sports as a form of exercise and way of sustaining morale. The servicemen played all types of sports like baseball and football. By this time the U.S. Army and the U.S. Navy had established dominant football programs that represented their respective academies. The Army-Navy game was one of college football's best rivalry games then as it is today and in many cases their games held national championship implications.

With the success of the military academy football teams, it was common for individual U.S. military bases and navy ships to establish their own football teams like the U.S. Marines of Key West and the U.S. Airforce "Flying Yanks". The football teams competed against other military squads as well as local university teams. In what could possibly be the first Cuban-American football game on record

The 1916 Army-Navy game, New York.

in 1906, the sailors of the USS *Columbia* played the University of Havana while stationed in the country. If there wasn't a team available to nearby, the military squad would divide into two and play a football game amongst themselves. Often times, the men played so physical that their superiors would order them to tone it down in fear of injuries.

These "military games" between servicemen weren't totally exclusive as they would usually allow anyone who wanted to play to participate including locals. For the Cubans that didn't know anything about American football, getting on the field was the quickest way to learn. After attaining a basic understanding of the game, the people would then teach others in the community how to play. For the younger Cubans football was an exciting new sport. The contact of the game and the fact that it is the polar opposite of baseball attracted many young men to play. It also helped that Cuban boys from an early age were raised *para ser macho* (to be macho). Football allowed them to display their masculinity to the opposite sex by playing the game courageously and strong. Soon, football became very popular with everyday Cubans. If there was a football around you can bet that a game was being played or going to be played. Eventually, the Cuban military became interested in football and they too went on to establish football teams.

James Hornibrook Kendrigan

Father of Cuban Football

Walter Camp is universally regarded as the "Father of American Football" for all his contributions as a player, coach, and innovator of the game. Though no one meant more to the overall game than Camp, James H. Kendrigan was Cuba's version of the late football great. Kendrigan was instrumental in establishing American football in Cuba and raising the sport's popularity all across the island. He was essentially the "Father of Cuban Football".

WHO WAS HE?

James "Jimmy" Hornibrook Kendrigan was born in September 1881 in Rockland, Massachusetts to Irish parents Thomas Francis Kendrigan, a constable police officer, and Mary Jane Kendrigan (Thompson). James, the eldest of four children, studied at Harvard and in-state Boston College. He was a halfback and captain of the Boston College football team in 1902. Kendrigan didn't play football at Harvard. While in his senior year at Boston College, Kendrigan established the Keewatin Academy for Boys, a college preparatory boarding school in the small town of Prairie du Chien, Wisconsin. Aside from being the founder, Kendrigan also served as a part-time headmaster at the all-boys school. Keewatin was advertised as a "direct preparatory to Harvard, Yale, Princeton, and the Massachusetts Institute of Technology" (College). Besides academics, it was

mandated that all the boys participate in sports. The students were taught various sports by coaches on the staff and the Keewatin's sports teams regularly competed against neighboring schools. The academy was a success and Kendrigan opened satellite campuses in other areas of Wisconsin as well as in Minnesota,

Michigan, and Ontario. In order to avoid the harsh winter months, Kendrigan established Keewatin campuses in Saint Augustine, Florida and in Havana, Cuba (College). For a small additional fee, students spent their midwinter term at these southern locations. Staying in Cuba offered a rare opportunity for students to learn about the Cuban culture and learn Spanish.

A NEW CAREER

Kendrigan decided that he wanted to venture into coaching athletics. While still the owner of Keewatin, he would no longer handle the school's day-to-day activities. In late-1902 he accepted the head coaching position to coach the Thorp's University football team in Louisville, Kentucky. Kendrigan was able to produce a good football team even with the school having a small enrollment. Next, he took over as the football coach at Detroit University School, a private boy's school that was similar to the academy that he founded. Kendrigan coached the Knights for two seasons, leading the squad to the national secondary championship game but ultimately coming up short against Lafayette High School from Buffalo, New York. After the two successful coaching stints, he decided to return to Keewatin Academy in 1914 to coach the football team. Kendrigan made the team into a powerhouse. Keewatin only had two loses in his 4 years as head coach. In 1921, he left Keewatin for a second time to take the same position at the Kentucky Military Institute. Besides football, Kendrigan coached track, baseball, and basketball at the majority of the schools as well.

THE CARIBES

Meanwhile in Havana, Cuban President Mario G. Menocal (pictured below) wanted to make all the University of Havana's sports teams more competitive especially football. Menocal had become in interested in football while studying at Cornell and later watching the sport as a member of the Vedado Tennis Club. Several years earlier, the Caribes football team played their first college football game against LSU. The Tigers demolished the Caribes in Havana 56-0. The embarrassingly lopsided defeat made it plainly obvious that the team was not ready to compete against American teams.

The LSU-Havana game being played at Almendares Park in Havana, Cuba 1907.

In 1923 President Menocal promoted Dr. Richard Grant, the school's track coach, to be the new director of athletics (Pérez). During the same time, Kendrigan was visiting the island as part of an athletic mission that was sponsored by sports writers. Upon hearing that Kendrigan was in town, Grant jumped at the opportunity to discuss the newly vacant Caribes head coaching position with Kendrigan. Having also coached track, Grant knew of Kendrigan by the success that he had with his track teams. Five of Kendrigan former track athletes would go on to compete in the 1920 Antwerp Olympics in Belgium with Frank Loomis taking home the gold medal for winning the men's 400-meter hurdles. The athletic director offered Kendrigan the football job and he accepted. As part of the contract, he was also to coach Havana's track, baseball, and basketball teams but his primary focus would be on the gridiron. Coach Kendrigan, known for his intense demeanor on the sidelines, was excited to take on the challenge. He described the Caribes football players as having a "great competitive spirit". He continued, "I've found the Cubans to be a fine type of athlete, well-disciplined despite their fiery nature" (Coached). After a short period assessing his new football team he realized that the team lacked organization. The blue-eyed Irish American would go on to rebuild the football program from the top to bottom but first he would have to start with the basics. Kendrigan taught the players about the rules of the football, he showed them how to practice, and other important facets of the game.

On July 1928, Kendrigan's athletic duties increased when he accepted the University of Havana athletics director job. He was the Caribes' head football coach and AD besides coaching other sports during the offseason. He held the dual positions for nearly 30 years. In 1952, Kendrigan suffered from an unknown life threatening disease and moved to Delvan, Illinois in order to be closer to family. James Kendrigan died a year later on July 14, 1953 at the age of 71.

LASTING LEGACY

Although Coach Kendrigan didn't have the success that he would have preferred with the football program, he did leave behind a lasting legacy. He was able to build interest around the Caribes football program in Cuba during a time in which the Cuban media often failed to cover the team because it was considered an "outsider" sport. Even with limited coverage Kendrigan was still able get locals excited about the Caribes' home games. Former Notre Dame great Knute Rockne was quoted by the Sunday Sentinel and Milwaukee Telegram as saying "interest in Havana seems to be growing by leaps and bounds". Rockne continued, "In the near future I look for the University of Havana to be able to give it to our best southern teams some real competition" (Rockne). Likewise, the Caribes football team was a large draw at games played in the United States. Their football games would often sellout and stadium crews had to add more seats to accommodate the expected crowd. The city of St. Petersburg, Florida found this out first hand in a November 29, 1929 that featured the University of Florida reserves. It was the largest attendance for a football game in the city's history at that time (Cuban).

As the athletic director, James Kendrigan tackled the University of Havana's lack of facilities problem. Kendrigan lobbied President Menocal for the school's much needed new stadium. The Caribes were playing football games at Almendares Park. The current Almendares Park, which replaced the original Almendares Park (1881-1916) that was several blocks away, was less than a decade old but it was already outdated and it was made specifically for baseball. The stadiums were located just outside old Havana, in the suburb of Almendares. Menocal approached local business leaders to help get funding for construction of UH's proposed stadium. Beer magnate Julio Blanco-Herrera generously offered to give the University of Havana the land and pay for the entire cost of the stadium. In October 1929, the University of Havana opened the mixed-use Gran Stadium Cervecería Tropical in the Havana borough of Marianao. The stadium was built on Blanco-Herrera's *Nueva Fábrica de Hielo* (New Ice Factory) grounds. Known by locals as La Tropical, after the Cuban beer of the same name that the factory produced, it was the best ballpark not just in the Havana but in the entire country. At the time, the stadium seated 12,000 and cost an estimated million dollars to build (Bennet). By today's standards it would put the stadium's total cost of construction at over $13 million. That was a ton of money back then but it was Julio Blanco-Herrera's way of giving back to the community.

The University of Havana Stadium, October 15, 1907.

In September 1945, James Kendrigan was able to convince longtime friend and future

College Football Hall of Fame coach Robert "Bob" Zuppke (pictured left) to take an unpaid assistant guest coach position at the University of Havana. The two became acquainted from their days as high school coaches in Illinois. Zuppke coached rival Oak Park and River High School to two state championships before taking the University of Illinois heading coaching job. "The Little Dutchman", as he was affectionately called, just finished a 28-year career with the Fighting Illini where he won 4 national championships and 7 Big Ten Conference titles. Several schools inquired about Zuppke's services but he declined their offers. Instead, he decided to move to Cuba to team up with old friend James Kendrigan and help coach the University of Havana freshman football team.

The coach was known for his aphoristic Zuppkeisms like "advice to freshmen: don't drink the liniment" and "alumni are loyal if a coach wins all his games" (Bob). Zuppke would need plenty of them as the majority of the players on the squad were entirely new to the sport of football. Though the coach faced many challenges, he looked forward to the change of setting. "He was overjoyed by the prospect of coaching, visiting Athletics Director James Kendrigan, and painting in the Cuban winter" (Brichford). In all reality Zuppke didn't need much convincing to move to Cuba. College football experts believed that his move was the start of his early retirement. Zuppke didn't want to retire quite yet from coaching though. His motivation for taking the job was that it came with a lot less pressure. With the team being so green there weren't any real expectations for the team. Plus, you can't beat living in tropical paradise after enduring many of Illinois' harsh winters.

'SELECT' SCHOOL FOR BOYS UNDER INQUIRY BY U. S.

Keewatin and 'Headmaster' Again in Grief.

Investigation of the activities of James Hornibrook Kendrigan, headmaster of Keewatin academy, an alleged exclusive school for boys on Sheridan road in Highland Park's residential district, will be launched today by federal authorities. It was announced yesterday by District Attorney Charles F. Clyne.

Two women probably will play important roles in the inquiry—one a leading blonde divorcee upon whom the headmaster is said to have lavished money and gifts and the other a British war widow who came to America to seek her fortune, was victimized by Kendrigan, it is said, and practically held a prisoner, penniless, in the north shore school.

Blonde Quits Hotel.

Mrs. Frances Van Sant Bennett, the noted haired divorcee from Chilli-the O. mysteriously disappeared

CLYNE EYES "SELECT" BOYS' SCHOOL

James Hornibrook Kendrigan, headmaster of Keewatin academy, who will have to explain his finan-

Frances Van S. Bennett, registrar of academy, a blonde divorcee

Mrs. Claire Smith, British widow, a teacher, who assu-

Home of Keewatin academy, Highland Park, which is said to be ed with firewood cut from trees in yard by boys, and the headm which James Hornibrook Kendrigan, is under scrutiny by Dis

*Keewatin Academy,
Highland Park, Illinois.*

SHADY PAST?

On December 13, 1922, the Chicago Tribune printed a damaging exposé on James Kendrigan and Keewatin Academy. Federal authorities launched an investigation on a wide range of different criminal activities that the former headmaster claimed to have committed. Some of the more serious charges against Kendrigan included embezzlement and false imprisonment. "A British war widow who came to America to seek her fortune, was victimized by Kendrigan, it is said, and practically held a prisoner, penniless, in the north shore school" (Select). Also, the newspaper alleged that Kendrigan moved the Keewatin Academy from location to location in order to avoid paying the mounting overdue rent bills. There were claims that he falsely advertised the school in order to get parents to enroll their sons at his school. Parents paid the $1,000 a year tuition while the boys weren't actually taught anything at the school (Select). The school itself was not the picturesque campus that it was portrayed to be. It was actually a residential home that was "almost devoid of furniture". "The boys have been compelled to sleep on the floors for nights at a time" (Select).

James Kendrigan, the man who would become the head coach for the Havana Caribes and essentially the "father of Cuban football", was using the sport as a vehicle to continue his illegal enterprise at Keewatin Academy. "Kendrigan imported a lot of football players by offering them money, free tuition, trips to Florida and other inducements to play on his eleven, advertise the school, and bring in gate receipts, which he pocketed" (Select).

Many of the football players, like the teachers at the school, were not paid. The players and teachers have since filed lawsuits against Kendrigan for unpaid wages.

Kendrigan was able to escape the "heat" back at home by accepting the job at the University of Havana. It is unclear if the university knew anything about Kendrigan's legal troubles when they hired him. While not much is known about the outcome of the federal investigations and pending lawsuits against him, Kendrigan did travel to the United States with the football team on a number of occasions. Furthermore, the U.S. and Cuba did have an existing extradition treaty at that time but Kendrigan was never arrested. It's safe to conclude that everything against him was eventually settled.

CHAPTER THREE

Football in its Infancy

Several months before Coach Kendrigan arrived on campus, the University of Havana Caribes played a football game against Rollins College, a private liberal arts school from Winter Park, Florida. The Tars obliterated the Caribes 80-0. "The Cubans were inexperienced and put up little opposition" (Rollins). Coach Kendrigan knew that he and his staff were going to have their work cut out for themselves. The Caribes football program was in complete despair and it was going to take a monumental makeover to turn the program around. Kendrigan was certainly up for the challenge and was determined to turn Havana into a perennial college football power.

By this time, the University of Havana had been playing football on and off for three decades but without any real coaches to teach the intricacies of the sport the players only had a limited knowledge of the game and its rules. It is hard to believe the how inept the football players were but it was a testament to how bad the coaching really was. Wearing his signature blue velvet fedora, the head coach held multiple scrimmages to assess his new football team. Football was played in a one-platoon system that required players to play on both offense and defense. Kendrigan watched how players pass, caught, defended, and tackled. The coach wasn't all too impressed with what he saw. Some of the assistant coaches joked that the players moved like they were dancing the rhumba. After going over the basics, he moved on to installing the offensive and defensive plays. The abundance of players left many players confused. The Cubans grew up playing baseball and unlike football there weren't any set plays that had to be memorized. While the Havana coaches would prefer a seasoned squad, there was a small silver lining to players being so inexperienced. The Caribes players haven't played enough football to create bad habits and the coaching staff could mold the young players to their liking.

The Caribes football players after practice (Kendrigran is in the background).

Fortunately for the coaches, they didn't have many problems communicating with their players as the majority of the team knew English. It allowed for all the football terminology to remain in English. This wasn't the case with Mexican football teams who spoke mainly Spanish and had to create a hodgepodge of English and Spanish-translated football terms. The Caribes went on to eventually develop a rivalry with the National Autonomous University of Mexico (UNAM) Pumas starting in late-1940s. As far as the Caribes coaching staff, they used their player's binguality to their advantage. When playing American opponents, the Caribes players were encouraged to speak Spanish so that their opponents won't be able to pick up on the play calls.

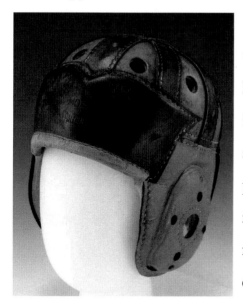

A similar helmet that is believed to have been worn by Gerald Ford while playing for the University of Michigan.

Kendrigan purchased new equipment for the team to replace the outdated equipment that they had been playing with. The football helmets were the biggest priority. By this time, leather came standard with protective padding on the inside to prevent violent blows to the head. The Caribes football team were playing with helmets that were more than 10 years old. "Kids used to get hurt easily. Those (leather) helmets--they had no foam inside or anything. You were better off playing without them" (DeSimone). During that time, wearing a football helmet was optional. Some players thought that it was too uncomfortable to wear so they commonly played without them. The NCAA made the use of the helmet mandatory in 1939.

The coaching staff tried to capitalize on the new direction of the Caribes football program by promoting the team to the community. Coach Kendrigan participated in numerous speaking engagements in hopes of getting more fans in the stands. The staff also visited local high schools to boost interest about the upcoming Caribes football games. Historically, the football team drew small crowds and admission to the games was free.

NEW SET OF RULES

College football had been using the forward pass since 1906 but the type of football that was played in Cuba was an old rugby-style game. Cuban teams only ran and never threw the ball. They were accustomed to playing football with the old rules because it was the way the game was played when it was first introduced in Cuba. The Cuban teams never adapted their game as football progressed. By the 1930s, American football had been using a longer, sleeker ball that had lacing to encourage passing. It was a change from the round rugby style ball that was used in the past. Even with all the changes, the Cuban football teams continued to play the game by the old set of rules.

Head coach Kendrigan brought a different philosophy of playing football the Havana Caribes. The team was now going to implement the forward pass in their offense. The

Caribes were becoming a passing football team. Havana's new passing offense would certainly help the Caribes players who were lighter and shiftier than their American counterparts. The team's average weight was only 160 lbs. By comparison, the national champion Michigan Wolverines were on average ten pounds heavier or so per player. The Cubans certainly weren't built for ground and pound style of football. Kendrigan believed that playing an aerial attack type offense would allow them to make plays in the open field and score more points. Knowing that his players weren't going to be bigger than their opponents, the Cubans had to be faster for them to be successful.

Even though the University of Havana were changing the way that they played, other Cuban teams like the Cuban Athletic Club and the Vedado Tennis Club continued to have no interest in passing. They opted to continue playing football by the old rules. Besides being stubborn, the club teams were known for their vicious gang tackling and the use of the flying wedge play which since became illegal in the sport. Modeled after an ancient military maneuver, the wedge was a v-shaped formation that was used to break through an opponent's line. The V, as it was commonly called, led to many injuries before being banned by college football. It was this type of play that led Columbia, Stanford, California, Georgia, and Georgia Tech to temporarily suspend their football programs

until new rules were implemented to make the game safer. The old rules versus new rules would eventually clash on the field when the Cuban Athletic Club played the University of Florida in 1912. More details about the game will be discussed in a later chapter.

PLAYER DEVELOPMENT

Kendrigan had plenty of head coaching experience on several levels but it was his ability to develop athletes that really set him apart from his coaching colleagues. Several of Kendrigan's former players went on to have much success in college and the pros like: Joe Guyon, John Barrett, and Francis "Fritz" Shiverick. Guyon, a Keewatin Academy product, went on to play halfback for Georgia Tech Golden Tornado (Yellow Jackets) and the New York Giants. Nicknamed the "Big Chief" because he was a Chippewa Indian, Guyon's play earned him entrance to both the College Football Hall of Fame and the Pro Football Hall of Fame. At the University of Havana, player development was almost nonexistent. Kendrigan knew that the Caribes players' strength was their quickness so he created a development program that focused exclusively on speed.

The main entrance of the University of Havana, circa 1950s.

This was a stark contrast to the college football norm of heavy weight training to bulk up. To do so he had to change their eating habits. The coach noticed that his players routinely ate breakfasts that consisted of eggs, toast, and *café con* (coffee with milk) with plenty of sugar. For lunch, it was black beans and rice along with some variation of meat. These types of heavy foods were banned by the coach for healthier options. Kendrigan advised his players to eat more greens and to drink several glasses of water between meals to stop the craving of more food. This diet would make the players leaner and faster on the football field. During practice, Coach Kendrigan didn't like for his players to drink water because he thought it would weaken their vitality. How times have changed! As college football has become more aware of the health of its players, Kendrigan would most certainly faced disciplinary actions today.

Cuban President Miguel Mariano Gómez

CHAPTER FOUR

A Powerful Ally

There was a new high ranking ambassador for football on the island when Miguel Mariano Gómez became the Cuba's president on May 20, 1936. Gómez, a self-described "sports fanatic", believed that participation in athletics led to sportsmanship and, in turn, created good citizens. His idea was based in part on Arthur Wellesley's adage "the battle of Waterloo was won on the fields of Eton" which suggests that participating in athletics creates many character building virtues. Competition fosters teamwork and respect, characteristics that are important for a nation's citizens. Competition also breeds champions. It is this athletic excellence that Gómez hopes will become a source of great Cuban nationalism. To achieve this, President Gómez devised a wide ranging amateur sports program to get all the citizens of Cuba involved in athletics.

THE BELOVED SON

Miguel Mariano Gómez was the son of José Miguel Gómez, Cuba's second president and one of the leaders of the Cuban War of Independence. The younger Gómez was expected to follow in his father's footsteps by one day serving in the country's highest

office but first he had to receive the proper education. Miguel was sent to study at the prestigious New York Military Academy in Cornwall-on-Hudson, New York. Gómez and also played football at the school. On Saturdays, Gómez attended Columbia University football games where his friend and fellow countrymen Carlos L. Henriquez Jr. played. Gómez became fast friends with Columbia head coach Luigi "Lou Little" Piccolo (pictured above). Gómez would eventually lean on both Little and Henriquez to help him carry out his vision for the country after he became president of Cuba.

Gómez returned home, graduated from the University of Havana Law School, and served successful terms in the Cuban House of Representatives and later as the mayor of Havana. Ever the diehard fan, it was said that Gómez had the Columbia football team's scores cabled to him as soon as the games were over. In 1935 he decided that the time was right to run for president. Gómez campaigned hard and won every province in a landslide general election victory the following year. After taking the oath of office,

President Gómez went right to work on his new national sports program. Interested in getting an American perspective, Gómez invited Little to Cuba so that the coach could speak to the leaders of the recently-formed Cuban athletic movement. Fresh off a season ending win against Stanford, Little was happy to assist his friend in any capacity that he could. Little spoke to the group about the different elements of developing and training various types of athletes including football players. While people of all ages should participate in sports, he stressed that the government pay particular attention to the country's youth. By teaching sports to the youth, they will be well positioned to influence their peers, families, and other people in the community to participate in athletics. The present youth will set the foundation of empowering future generations of Cuban athletes.

THE PROGRESSION OF FOOTBALL

Fulgencio Batista, an Army Colonel at the time, was enthusiastic about the president's plan and ordered the Cuban military to establish football teams. The *Marina de Guerra Constitucional de Cuba* (Cuban Constitutional Navy), the Cuban Army, Cuban Marines, the Cuban Military Academy, and the Morro Castle Military Academy all formed teams. The Cuban Military Academy's 35-man football team was made up of a mix of army and navy cadets. The Cuban National Police formed a football squad as well. The military and police teams never had quality coaches and hence weren't all that competitive. These teams mostly played football games amongst themselves and rarely scheduled games against American opponents.

Batista (pictured right) sent soldiers to schools to teach boys and girls how to play various sports. They taught the kids the importance of physical training and being part of a larger team. At the time, the colonel was working on an independent rural education program that he devised. The program involved building schools in rural areas and assigning servicemen to teach at the schools. Illiteracy was high amongst the *guajiros* (farmers) that lived outside of Cuba's major cities. President Gómez's national sports program and Batista's rural education program were a great match. They both used education as way to empower the Cuban people

so that they could live better lives. In turn, the citizens will raise the country's international profile to more respectability.

It wasn't just the rural schools that benefited, the military sent soldiers to Cuba's larger cities as well. Havana, Santa Clara, Camagüey, and as far east as Santiago de Cuba received an infusion of new soldier-teachers. One of the better known Cuban football players to benefit from the sports program was Darío Guitart-Manday. Darío first learned to play football at a secondary school called the Institute of Havana (IH). After graduating from the high school (later renamed Pre-University Institute José Martí) he attended the University of Havana and played on the Caribes football team. He played quarterback and halfback for coach Bob Zuppke. While Guitart-Manday was only 146 lbs., he was fast and was exactly what Zuppke was looking for to run the T formation offense. It was called the "T" because three halfbacks were positioned behind the quarterback forming the shape of the letter.

Regular formation showing the position for every man to assume.   *Photo by Lyndon.*

Darío's ability to play both quarterback and halfback made him perfect fit for the offense. He became the star of the Caribes team with performances like the one he had in a game

against the Miami Naval Training Center team in the Orange Bowl in which he scored every way possible including a kickoff return. The former quarterback went on to have successful coaching stints with several military football teams before starting a career as an ichthyologist (fish biologist).

Coach Zuppke had a special eye for talent. He once coached Ernest Hemingway at Oak Park High School in 1916. Hemingway played right guard for the school's lightweight football team. Zuppke always thought that his former player would go on to have a great career, the future Nobel Laureate did but not in football. Interestingly, Ernest Hemingway was living in Havana as an expatriate when Zuppke was hired to coach the Caribes. The two met for the first time in 29 years since their days at Oak Park High. The two remained close friends ever since.

Cuban President Miguel Mariano Gómez's national sports program encouraged the formation of organized football leagues on the island. The Cuban Amateur Football Federation was one such league. The league had eight teams that consisted of American and Cuban players.

Athletic clubs like the Vedado Tennis Club and the Cuban Athletic Club joined the league as did the existing military football teams. The newcomers were the Miramar Yacht Club and the Havana Yacht Club. Even with increased competition, the CAC were no match for the other teams. The Tigers held the national champion title the majority of the time.

Though it was a billed as a semi-pro football league, it was technically still considered amateur competition since the players were not paid. President Gómez wanted the sports program to foster amateur competition rather than professional. Cuba never had a professional football league on the island. Several decades later, future Cuban leader Fidel Castro had similar sentiments about the type of athletics that should be played in the country. Castro went on to abolish all professional sports on the island.

CHAPTER FIVE

Cuba Loves to Host

Ever since the early 20th century Havana was known as America's playground. While Havana was a "foreign" city, it wasn't completely unfamiliar to many Americans. Americans first experienced the "Paris of the Caribbean" starting with the U.S. military occupation after Cuba gained their independence and later with Havana's American-focused tourism industry. The city's close proximity to the United States and their relaxed attitude made it a favorite tourist destination for travelers. Starting in the 1920s, new restaurants, hotels, nightclubs, and golf courses sprang up all across Havana. Sloppy Joe's Bar and El Floridita became favorite watering holes for celebrities like Ernest Hemingway, John Wayne, Clark Gable, and Ava Gardner. Cuban officials wanted to capitalize on the American interests so they turned their attention to sports, including college football.

THE FESTIVAL

Fresh off a pre-inaugural visit to the United States in April 1936, incumbent Cuban President Miguel Mariano Gómez wanted his country to host a series of American sporting events as a way to bolster strained relations with its neighbor to the north. It was to be an extension of the national sports program that he established. Gómez appointed friend Carlos Henriquez Jr. as the Commissioner of Cuban Sports and director of the sports festival. Henriquez had thorough knowledge of American sports. Aside from playing football, he was also the captain of the Columbia wrestling team.

The Cuban government announced a week long Cuban National Sports Festival starting on Christmas Day in 1936. The festival will feature 56 different sporting events. "Approximately 300 athletes, more than 200 from the United States, will participate. Among the sports are football, baseball, basketball, boxing, track, tennis, polo, swimming, wrestling and Jai Alai" (Havana). As an incentive to attract tourists, Cuban hotels gave guests a gold key that could be redeemed for one free drink at every bar in town. The offer of free boozes was enticing for many Americans. Prohibition ended several years earlier in the United States but there were still "dry" regions that prohibited the purchase of alcohol.

LET THE GAMES BEGIN

The event opened with a game between the Cuban Marines and the Cuban Athletic Club. The highlight of the day though belonged to James "Jesse" Owens. With less than

4 months removed since taking home four gold medals in the 1936 Berlin Olympics, Owens participated in two separate events. The Buckeye Bullet ran a 100-meter dash against a stopwatch to see if he could break his own world record. Unfortunately, the wet conditions didn't allow him to reach the mark. In the second event, he ran another 100-meter sprint but this time he raced a champion racehorse named Julio McCaw. McCaw was considered the fastest thoroughbred in all of Cuba. Officials gave Owens a 40-yard advantage and he would use the lead to beat the chestnut steed and his jockey J.M. Contino by 20-yards or so. Both races took place during the halftime of the Cuban Marines-Cuban Athletic Club game. After the race, football players from both squads along with fans swarmed around Owens in excitement. With everyone on the field, the start of the third quarter was delayed. Cuban soldiers quickly intervened to restore order and get the group off of the field. The football game commenced and the Cuban Athletic Club beat the marines 7-6. The CAC were led to victory by advisory head coach Harvey Harman.

Coach Harvey Harman shortly after arriving in Cuba.

Harman agreed to the coach the Cuban team after the college football season was over. He coached the University of Pennsylvania Quakers to a 7-1 record and a No. 10 ranking in the Associated Press Poll. Harman was later posthumously inducted into the College Football Hall of Fame. Another interesting caveat about the game, the University of Miami Hurricanes were due to face the Cuban Athletic Club but scheduling conflicts didn't allow the game to come to fruition. It would have been the first meeting between the two clubs.

The next several days were filled with various athletic events. For the Cuban National Sports Festival's grand finale, a collegiate football game that featured two of America's best teams- the Alabama Polytechnic Institute (Auburn University) and Villanova University. The Auburn-Villanova matchup will be played on New Year's Day at La Tropical Stadium in Havana. The stadium, who now seats 30,000, was considered to be enlarged to hold 50,000 for the game but the upgrade proved to be too costly and it was never came to fruition. Several schools including: Marquette, Pittsburgh, Temple, Alabama, LSU, Duke, Tennessee, Pennsylvania, Arkansas, and George Washington were invited to play the exhibition game against Auburn. Auburn agreed to play after negotiating a $15,000 guarantee along with a promise of more from game receipts. Many people believed that the undefeated the Marquette University Golden Avalanche were a shoo-in to face Auburn but Villanova ultimately accepted the invitation first. Instead, Marquette accepted the challenge to play in the inaugural Cotton Bowl Classic against Texas Christian University (TCU). The TCU Horned Frogs won the contest 16-6.

The Auburn-Villanova matchup provided several good storylines. It was the first postseason game for both squads and the first ever meeting between the Tigers and Wildcats. Also, the game will reunite the head coaches Jack Meagher and Maurice "Clipper" Smith who were teammates on Knute Rockne' 1919 Notre Dame Co-National Championship Team (there wasn't a clear cut winner and the NCAA lists Centre,

Harvard, Illinois, and Texas A&M as the other shared champions). The winner of the Auburn-Villanova game will be presented with the newly-created President's Cup.

Villanova coach Clipper Smith (left) and Auburn coach Jack Meager (right).

While Henriquez was enthusiastic about the upcoming gridiron game, he didn't want it to be a "bowl game" in the traditional sense. The overall goal of the Cuban National Sports Festival was to promote interest in American sports in Cuba. He believed that creating a "bowl" type game will only limit Cuba's involvement to merely being the host country. Instead, Henriquez envisioned a "defender-challenger" model with the winner of the inaugural game defending their President's Cup against a challenging future American football opponent. Eventually, Henriquez would like a Cuban team game to participate in the annual game.

The football game was going to provide plenty of meaningful exposure to island nation. It was broadcasted via radio within Cuba and in the United States by the Mutual Broadcasting Company. As talk of the game spread by the press and college football fans alike, the game was dubbed the "Bacardi Bowl" by some and "Rhumba Bowl" by others. It's safe to say that Henriquez wasn't all too pleased with the game's unofficial nicknames that were being floated around.

Former Cuban President José Miguel Gómez (left), Harvey Harman (middle), and Carlos L. Henriquez Jr. (right).

Villanova head coach Clipper Smith (left) shaking hands with and Carlos L. Henriquez Jr. (right).

"THE BACARDI BOWL"

1/1/1937

It was the day of the game and it was a revolutionary atmosphere. With a heavy Cuban military presence, it felt more like the players were going into actual battle than playing a football game. The visionary of the event, Miguel Mariano Gómez was ousted as president several days earlier. Batista, a one-time comrade, led the charge to Gómez's impeachment. Gómez requested to U.S. President Franklin D. Roosevelt that he intervene in the matter but the president refused. After less than a year in office, he was ousted as Cuba's president. The football game would be Gómez's final public

appearance. As part of the agreement, Gómez was to leave the country that night. He was to be immediately replaced by Vice-President Federico Laredo Brú. While Brú was Cuba's new president, it was really self-appointed Chief of the Military Fulgencio Batista who was the country's de facto leader. With 15,000 to 18,000 people in the stands, the 2:30 p.m. game drew a

The captains- Villanova's Tony Sala (left) and Walter Gilbert (right) of Auburn.

The Wildcats trying to run the football.

quarter of the fans that were expected. Auburn, led by 1935 SEC Coach of the Year Jack Meagher, was the first to strike when Tigers' halfback Billy Hitchcock broke a tackle for a 40-yard touchdown in the first quarter. Hitchcock later told the press, "It was hot as the devil out there. Batista [future] Cuban dictator showed up four or five minutes into the first half. There was a tremendous roar that went up from the crowd. We didn't know what was going on, but we had to stop playing because of the noise" (Plott). The game commenced as the fans waved white handkerchiefs in the stands to show their support of Batista. Back on the field, the game was all about the defenses. Both defensive lines made it nearly impossible to run the football. Soon things got a little chippy. Villanova guard Joseph Missar and Auburn's Sam McCrocksey got into a fight in the second quarter. Both players threw punches and were ejected from the game.

Villanova on offense and looking to score.

An Auburn defender making a tackle.

The officials that were hired to work the game were veteran referee Wilmer Crowell, former Georgia star James "Buck" Cheves, and one-time Georgia Tech National Champion George "Pup" Philips. After being dominated the majority of the game, Villanova head coach "Clipper" Smith told his team to keep on battling. In the second half, the Wildcats made some key defensive stops to keep the Wildcats within a touchdown. Late in the fourth quarter, the Tigers were punting deep in their territory. Villanova's John Wysocki and Valentine Rizzo were able to block the punt. The ball fell to the ground around the two-yard line and Wildcat lineman Matthew Kuber picked up the loose ball and ran in for the touchdown. William Christopher kicked the important extra point. Time winded down and the game finished in a 7-7 tie. Overtime didn't exist at this time in football and games commonly ended in draws (college football introduced overtime 60 years later). The Tigers and Wildcats ended the 1936 football season with nearly identical records, 7-2-2 and 7-2-1 respectively.

The game was almost cancelled before it even began. Unhappy that his picture wasn't featured in the game's program, Fulgencio Batista ordered that the game not be played. The programs were reprinted with the added photo and the game was allowed to be played as scheduled (Walsh). The new government regime didn't have any interest continuing Miguel Mariano Gómez sports program. As a result, the annual football series ended with this single football game. It was the first and last state-sponsored game of its kind. Shared winners Auburn and Villanova were the only teams to ever be awarded the President's Cup.

There was a growing anti-American sentiment amongst many Cubans under Federico Laredo Brú's administration. Many Cubans were living in poverty and they began to resent Americans as they lavishly vacationed in their country. For the Cubans, the "Yankees" were exploiting Havana's unattainable Cuban pleasures. Cubans urged the government to rid the country of American interests and its dependency from its neighbors. While individual Cuban teams continued to play American schools, the growing anti-American sentiment didn't bode well for future college football bowl games to be hosted in the island. By 1937, college football had five major bowl games: The Rose Bowl in Pasadena, the Festival of Palms Bowl (Orange Bowl) in Miami, the Sugar Bowl in New Orleans, the Sun Bowl in El Paso, and the Cotton Bowl Classic in Dallas. College football decision makers talked about Havana possibly hosting the sixth major college bowl game. The city certainly met all the criteria. Havana is a warm climate city, it is relatively easy to travel to, and it had a built-in infrastructure for the visitors that were going to travel to attend the game. With too many obstacles in their path and the possibility of losing a ton of money, investors balked at the idea of making a college football bowl game in Havana.

CHAPTER SIX

Abolishment of the Sport

The next four years under Cuban President Federico Brú's were relatively uneventful in regards to football. The president did host longtime friend and Penn State head coach Robert "Bob" Higgins in April 1939. Higgins once played professionally for the NFL's Canton Bulldogs and was later inducted into the College Football Hall of Fame as a coach in 1954. The two met while as classmates at the Peddie School in New Jersey and they continued to remain close friends (Kurtz). Led by a military escort, the Nittany Lions coach was taken to the presidential palace in Brú's private car where a reception was held in Higgins honor (Kurtz). The reunion was just a get-together amongst two friends, it wasn't to discuss potential football games between Penn State and Havana.

NEW LEADERSHIP

Fulgencio Batista took office on October 10, 1940 and served two intermittent terms sandwiched between two marginal Cuban presidents. The second term, which began twelve years later, wasn't exactly a democratic process. Batista staged a military coup, cancelled presidential elections, and became the dictator of Cuba. The son of peasant farmers, Batista wasn't interested in improving Cuban society. His motivation as president was predicated around money and power. Batista's reign was marked with corruption on all levels and plundering for his own financial gain. Cuba became a haven for prostitution, drugs, and gambling. Meyer Lansky, a well-known Mafia associate and longtime friend of Batista, soon ran Havana's casinos and racetracks. Lansky also bought the Hotel Nacional de Cuba and the Hotel Habana Riviera to rake in money from their casinos. At one point, the casinos in Havana were making as much money as the casinos in Las Vegas. Not to be left out, Batista received kickbacks from all gambling operations along with essentially every government contract in the country. In 1958, Baltimore Colts owner Carroll Rosenbloom wanted in on the action so he purchased the 457-room Hotel Nacional from Lanskey. Known for being a high-stake gambler, Rosenbloom was taken a big chance on the luxury hotel that was famously known for hosting the Havana Conference- a summit of the day's best known mobsters. The Havana Conference was depicted in Francis Ford Coppola's film *The Godfather Part II*. During the filming of the movie, Cuba was already off-limits to Americans. The scene was subsequently shot at the Occidental El Embajador in Santo Domingo, Dominica Republic. The purchase would later prove to be the wrong bet for Rosenbloom as a socialist-leaning lawyer turned rebel leader Fidel Castro was emerging on the political landscape.

AN UPRISING

Several years earlier, Fidel Castro (right) was studying law at the University of

Havana. Besides academics, he was a pitcher on the Caribes baseball team and was heavily involved in Cuban politics on campus. Castro became a member of the campus-based socialist group the People's Party. The group were staunch critics of the "imperialistic" Unites States and opposed all U.S. involvement in the Cuba. It was a sentiment that Castro continued after eventually coming into power. In February 1948, Castro was

midway through his law studies when he was reportedly involved in the murder of Manuel "Manolo" de Castro Campo (no relation to Fidel). Campo was the leader of a rival student political group and a former University of Havana football player. Castro was subsequently arrested and questioned for the murder but it is believed that his father paid off authorities for Fidel's release. Manolo's murder continues to remain unsolved.

In mid-1955, there was a growing disdain with the Batista administration. Three years into the president's second term, many Cubans wanted a change in the country's leadership. The university became the epicenter for political protests. Professors and students united and regularly held anti-Batista demonstrations. A large portion of the

18,000 UH student body rallied around Castro who recently graduated from the school and formed a guerilla army to overtake Batista. On campus, the protests started peaceful but quickly turned violent. Fights and stabbings regularly took place between Batista and Castro supporters. Due to the escalating violence, the University of Havana governing council ordered the school be closed on November 20, 1956. The university would remain closed for the next two and a half years. Meanwhile, the Havana Caribes football team was scheduled to face Stetson in Havana in less than two weeks. Initially scheduled to play in Havana, the ongoing war caused the game to be moved to Key West, Florida. The Caribes played Stetson 10 days after the university was ordered to be shut down. The Cuban team unknowingly played their last football game. The game marked the end of football in Cuba.

With the university closed, students took to the streets to continue protesting. Caribes football player José Antonio Echeverría was one such protester. Echeverría formed a militant group and took a radio station to spread an anti-Batista message over the national airwaves. He was gunned down by Cuban police after the incident. Ignacio Reyes Murillo, a teammate of Echeverría's said, "On the university team, there were men who died fighting Batista and men who died fighting Castro" (DeSimone).

Batista would ultimately lose the support from the U.S. government and the military had trouble fending off the rebels. After 25 months of war, Batista felt the pressure of defeat and fled Cuba. Fidel Castro became the country's new leader.

A DIFFERENT CUBA

With Fidel Castro now as Cuba's communist dictator, the government began to rid itself of all American interests. American assets were seized and became property of the state. An estimated $1.85 billion in money and property was confiscated from U.S. citizens by the Cuban government (Foreign). The Cuban people were also victimized. Cuban companies, businesses, and land were nationalized. The Bacardi company, who initially supported Castro during the war, now became government property. As a result of the mass repossessions, Americans and Cubans fled the island in droves, essentially leaving behind whatever property that they had left. Next, the government turned their attention to schools and country clubs. Private schools like Colegio de Belén where Fidel and his brother Raúl studied were ordered to be closed. Also, social clubs were deemed illegal. The clubs' American-educated bourgeoisie members were considered a direct contradiction to the new Cuban government communist ideals. The Vedado Tennis Club and Cuban Athletic Club ceased and with it their football teams. The clubhouses became government property. The VTC clubhouse was renamed the "José Antonio Echeverría Social Circle" and was made into a Cuban baseball museum. Other clubhouses were used as military bases.

The Vedado Tennis Club today.

In July 1959, the University of Havana was reopened but notably absent was the Caribes football team. Castro banned football not just at the university but in the entire country. Football was a sign of "Yankee imperialism" and it was supposedly everything against what the new revolutionary government stood for. There was more to the football ban than what the government let on. Castro didn't ban baseball even though the it is an American sport. In fact, baseball became the national symbol of the Revolution. Fidel even played in an exhibition game with his own team *Los Barbudos* (the Bearded Ones) against the Cuban military police team. "Castro pitched and had two strikeouts in two innings" (Elias). Castro proclaimed, "Our revolution has established the principle whereby sport is a right of the people, and we could add that sport is also a duty of the people..." (Cuba). Baseball, unlike football, was an Olympic sport and winning on the international level was a way of legitimizing their government to the rest of the world. If football was a medal winning sport, there is a possibility that the game would still be played on the island today. Like President Gómez's idea of the national sports program two decades earlier, Castro would also use sports to encourage Cuban patriotism. He developed the National Institute of Sport, Physical Education, and Recreation (INDER) program. INDER was a comprehensive physical education and athletic program that was accessible to the whole population. Citizens were expected to participate in sports from an early age. All sports are encouraged except for football of course.

CHAPTER SEVEN

Renewed Interest?

On December 17, 2014 U.S. President Barack Obama and Cuban President Raúl Castro jointly announced that there will be a thawing in U.S.-Cuba relations. Raúl became Cuba's president six years earlier after his older brother Fidel stepped down due to health issues. While out of the limelight, Fidel remains a staunch critic of the United States and does not fully agree with his brother's decision of easing relations with their Cold War for. Obama visited Cuba in March 2016. He became the first sitting U.S. president to visit the island in over 85 years. On the final day of the 3-day visit, the two leaders enjoyed a baseball game that featured the Tampa Bay Rays and the Cuban National Team at

U.S. President Barack Obama and Cuban President Raul Castro watching the baseball game, March 22, 2016.

Estadio Latinoamericano (Latin American Stadium) in Havana. The Rays won 4-1. Coincidentally, the stadium was once used for political rallies before the Revolution. The late José Antonio Echeverría once used the location to protest for change.

A CITY IN MOTION

In 2003, a pair of San Diego, California high school football teams traveled to Havana to play a football game. It was the season opener for the Bonita Vista Barons and the La Jolla Vikings. More importantly, it was the first football game that was played in the island since the Cuban Revolution. The game was a homecoming for Bonita Vista coach Carl Parrick. Carl and his family lived in Cuba as his Navy lieutenant father was stationed in the country. They lived in a neighborhood that was called the Country Club Nuevo Biltmore. When Castro took power the Parrick family moved stateside. The coach recalled, "We had to flee and leave everything we owned one morning at about 2 in the morning" (Fiorina). Parrick was elated to be back and even had the chance to visit his old home during the trip. The players and coaches were like ambassadors of the sport. The football players visited local schools to generate student interest in the game while the football coaches conducted clinics to give the Cubans a crash course on football. One of the schools that was visited was the University of Havana. By this time, it has been nearly 50 years since the Caribes had a football team. Some of the Cuban students said that they were interested in reestablishing a team.

The game was publicized by the Cuban Sports Ministry as the "Havana Classic". Radio, television, and newspaper announcements could be heard asking the public to attend the free game at Cuba's national soccer stadium Estadio Nacional de Fútbol Pedro Marrero (formerly the La Tropical). About 400 spectators showed us to watch Bonita Vista-La Jolla football game. Several former Caribes players like Rafael Hernandez Rousseau were in attendance. While most Cubans didn't understand the rules of the game, it didn't matter, they still had plenty of fun. The length of the field was shortened to 90 yards due to the field conditions but no one noticed anyways. Bonita Vista went on to beat La Jolla 31-22. After the game, players handed out 500 footballs to the fans in attendance. Some of the fans even asked the high school players for their autographs.

THE MAD HATTER

In March 2016, LSU head football coach Les Miles (pictured below) visited Cuba. While the university said that it was a personal vacation, his visit did have some political undertones. President Obama had recently announced the normalization process with Cuba and was scheduled to visit the country. Coincidently, Miles and Obama arrived in Cuba less than an hour apart. It's uncertain if the two met but they did attend the baseball game. Coach Miles visited local schools, ate at restaurants, and soaked in the

Cuban culture. He even tossed around a football with locals. Miles thoroughly enjoyed his 5-day visit but did provide some criticism. "It was not necessarily comfortable, there's some things they have to do. . . older cars, older buildings that need some work, but the people are pretty special" (Kleinpeter).

Prior to the coach's arrival, Miles sent the University of Havana a signed football to commemorate the LSU-Havana game that was played in 1907. The football was inscribed "To our friends in Havana Geaux Tigers! Les Miles". The University of Havana appreciated the gesture as the football is now on display at the university's trophy room. It is a tiny reminder of the university's forgotten history of playing college football.

THE NFL

The National Football League has longed to promote its brand internationally after the NFL Europe folded. The European-based developmental football league comprised of teams from Canada, Germany, Netherlands, Spain, United Kingdom, and the U.S. Marketed as the "NFL International Series", the league changed its focus to NFL teams playing games in foreign cities. The NFL held games in Mexico and England. "The largest crowd for a regular season game occurred on Oct. 2, 2005 when the San Francisco 49ers played the Arizona Cardinals at Azteca Stadium in Mexico City. That game drew 103,467 fans who witnessed the first-ever regular season game played outside the United States" (Cowboys). The record was later eclipsed but it remains second largest attendance of all-time. There are more international games that are scheduled for the future. The NFL is also considering unfamiliar markets for possible games. According to Bleacher Report NFL Insider Jason Cole, the NFL is considering the idea of playing a football game in Havana. "The thinking behind hosting a game in Cuba is that it would be a 'historic game' and possibly bridge relationships between the two countries" (NFL). Whether a game will be eventually played in the tiny island nation remains to be seen but with the big money that will be involved cash-strapped Cuba would most likely jump at the opportunity.

NEW GENERATION OF FOOTBALL FANS

Not long ago the only places where American television could be watched was at expensive internet cafés and hotels that were restricted for tourists. The government has since lifted the ban on off-limit hotels. That combined with the illegal satellite dishes that are present in many homes, more and more Cubans are tuning in to American sports including football. While older Cubans stick to watching baseball, the younger people search out for "exotic" sports to watch. Football has become popular to watch. Even though most don't understand the basic rules of the game, they still have a rooting interest. When asked, most Cubans would say that they are Miami Dolphins fans (proximity to the country) or a fan of the team that most recently won the Super Bowl. The increasing accessibility is only going to continue to fuel their passion for the sport.

CHAPTER EIGHT

Memorable Games

The football games in this chapter are some of the most notable games. It is by no means a complete list of all the games. Refer to Appendix A for a list of the games and outcomes.

11/24/1906

This date is significant in that it could possibly be the first time that a Cuban football team played an American opponent. The University of Havana faced the servicemen from the USS *Columbia*. "The sailors were too heavy for the students and won the game by a score of 15 to 0" (Other). It is presumed that the navy team scored 3 touchdowns to get their 15-point total as each touchdown scored as 5 points during that time. Teams wouldn't bother with the extra point if the goalposts weren't present. Interestingly, the high speed protector cruiser was the flagship of the North Atlantic Squadron and was stationed in Cuba during the Spanish-American War. The USS *Columbia* was decommissioned in June 1921.

This Christmas Day was an historic day that provided many firsts for both the NCAA and LSU football. LSU became the first college football team to play an opponent on foreign soil that wasn't in Canada. The game was dubbed "The Bacardi Bowl" after the Cuban spirits maker (Bacardi didn't actually sponsor the game). Led by first year head coach Edgar R. Wingard, it was also the Tigers' first bowl game in their history.

The 1907 LSU Tigers football team, coach Wingard on the far left.

The Tigers dominated the University of Havana 56-0 in front of 10,000 fans. "Almendares Park was filled with Cuban government officials, Havana high society and plenty of very enthusiastic American servicemen" (Vincent). Most Cubans couldn't afford the $10 ticket to the game which was considered a large back then. It is also noteworthy to mention that future LSU Hall of Famer and College Football Hall of Famer George "Doc" Fenton scored the game's first touchdown (Doc). The highlight of the game though went to John Seip, the Tigers' starting end, who ran back a 67-yard punt return for a touchdown (Vincent). LSU fans didn't have any doubts that the Tigers were going to win the game. It was said that fans raised $2,000 so that team officials could wager on the game for them.

Game action between the Tigers and the Caribes.

While the atmosphere at the game was jovial, it was more tense outside of the stadium. It had been less than a decade after the Spanish–American War and remnants of the war could be seen throughout the city like the USS *Maine*. The wrecked steel warship was still visible in the Havana Harbor when LSU players arrived.

Shortly after taking the Tulane heading coaching job, Joe Curtis scheduled a future game against the Cuban Athletic Club. The national media called the international intercollegiate game a publicity stunt. In the beginning of 1909 Curtis decided to retire but still consulted succeeding head coach Robert "Buster" Brown. Curtis said, "He [Buster] will have a good team this fall to tackle the Cubans" (Grigg). It was also reported that the Tulane coaches were so confident in winning the game that they didn't feel the need for their players to practice very much (Joe Curtis). Their laissez-faire approach would certainly come back to haunt them.

The 1909 Tulane Olive and Blue football team.

The 1909 CAC Tigers football team.

L. PLATT

COACH Y FULL BACK

M. GASTAÑEDA

LEFT HALF BACK Y MANAGER

F. LAVANDEIRA

CAPITAN Y RIGHT END

The CAC Tigers outplayed the Olive and Blue from start to finish and held them team scoreless for a 11-0 win. The game marked the first victory that a Cuban team had over an American opponent. The surprising underdog victory made national news in Cuba and in the U.S. Tulane would finish the season 4–3–2 but the sting from the postseason bowl loss proved to be Brown's undoing. He was fired after just one season at the helm.

1/1/1912

For the Mississippi A&M (Mississippi State) Aggies, the 1911 football season ended with a final game against an unfamiliar foe, in unfamiliar territory. They were to play the Cuban Athletic Club in Havana, Cuba. The 1911 season was the last year that a touchdown was scored as 5 points in college football. It was to be changed to the now familiar 6 points the following season.

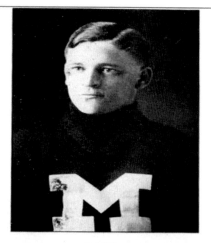

BASS.
"Corporal" was a terror to the opposing back field. As an end, he always tried to do a little more than his share. Victory or defeat, he never let up. He played a most brilliant game against Auburn and L. S. U. He is of All-Southern caliber.

The Aggies had a successful 6–2–1 season and were looking forward to their postseason game in the tropical city. The game didn't come without tragedy. On a prior game against Birmingham College on November 3, the Aggies starting right end Levy "Corporal" Bass suffered a routine injury during the game. Following the game, the injury quickly developed into spinal meningitis and the disease soon spread throughout his body. On December 17, Bass succumbed to the disease two weeks before the Aggies' scheduled game against the Cuban football club (Cote). Still reeling from the Bass' sudden passing, the coaching staff and players had a team meeting on whether they should play their final game. The Aggies players decided to play the game so that they could honor Bass. A&M's head coach W.D. "Billy" Chadwick didn't make the trip so that he could attend the funeral. Chadwick appointed assistant and future A&M head coach Earle C. "Billy" Hayes as the interim head coach (Cote).

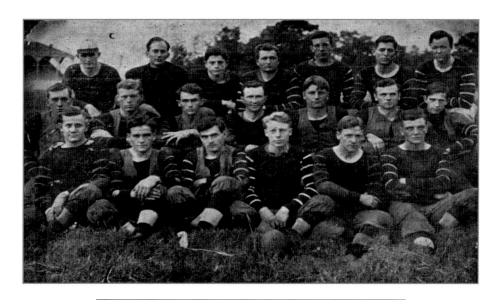

The 1911 Mississippi A&M Aggies football team.

With a new coach leading the team, veteran starting halfback Morley "Jopsey" Jennings felt like he had to be the team's catalyst. The 170 lb. Jopsey gave a dominant performance and it was his play which propelled the team to a 12-0 win. Jopsey would eventually enter the College Football Hall of Fame as a coach but he is more known by Mississippi State fans as being the school's first four-sport athlete. He also participated in baseball, basketball, track besides football. At the time, the school's yearbook Reveille nicknamed the 1911 football team the "bull dogs" for the fight that the team displayed on the field. The school would officially adopt the Bulldogs mascot for all of their athletics teams in 1961.

12/28/1912

The University of Florida traveled to Havana in December 1912 to play a two game series against different Cuban athletic clubs. The first game went off without a hitch and the newly-named Gators football team pounded the Vedado Tennis Club 27-0 on Christmas Day. The same couldn't be said three days later when the Gators faced the Cuban Athletic Club at the same venue Almendares Park in Havana. The host team normally determined which set of rules the teams were going to play by. The CAC and the Gators agreed beforehand that the game would be played with the new rules. "The Florida players complained that the Cubans persisted in playing under the old rules"

Actual game day program (left).

The 1912 Vedado Marqueses football team.

(Football). Also, Gator's head coach George E. Pyle (right) didn't like the way that game was being officiated. "According to one source, the game's referee was a former coach for the Cuban team, and the officiating was blatantly biased. After two Florida touchdowns were nullified by questionable officiating, Pyle protested a fifteen-yard penalty. When the referee offered a five-yard penalty instead, Pyle and his team left the game in protest" (Conner). Meanwhile, the spectators were unhappy that the game was suspended and the police were called. Pyle

was questioned and subsequently arrested. "He was taken into custody by the police on the charge of violating a Cuban law forbidding the suspending of a game for which gate money has been charged" (Football). Coach Pyle was then released from jail and was to be arraigned on a later date with the promise that he would appear in court. George Pyle didn't wait around to face his charge in court, he and his team boarded a ferry traveled back home. The coach, who would later become the athletic director of the West Virginia Mountaineers, was branded by the Cuban government a "fugitive of justice" (Conner). The referees declared the Tigers the winners due to Florida's forfeiture. The loss dropped Florida's record to 5-3-1 but 1-2 in 25-member Southern Intercollegiate Athletic Association (SIAA) conference. More importantly, the incident placed serious doubts on whether the two teams will meet again in the future.

The Stetson University Hatters finished their 1919 regular football season with a 4-3 record before their scheduled postseason bowl game. They were set to face the Cuban Athletic Club on New Year's Day. Stetson fired longtime head coach Litchfield Colton and didn't allow him to coach bowl. Colton was also an engineering professor at Stetson. The athletic director brought in H.T. (Pug) Allen as his replacement.

After a grueling trip from Central Florida that included rides from a bus, train, and ferry the Hatters team finally arrived to Havana on New Year's Eve. The Hatters football team lodged at the Hotel Brooklyn, a hotel that was commonly frequented by American tourists (Oshihiyi). The hotel was located on Paseo de Martí in historic Old Havana. That night, some members of the CAC took the American team sight-seeing and some late-night fun. They visited every tourist sport that was worth seeing in the city.

"The last place of interest that we [Hatters players] were introduced to was the cemetery. The Cubans seemed to think that it was a great joke to take us there before the game" (Oshihiyi). Meanwhile, the rest of Havana was out celebrating the start of the impending

1920 New Year. Former Stetson player, Grant "Spider" Wilbanks described the scene as such, "The New Year celebration was wild by American standards, and included whistles, guns, firecrackers and cars' backfiring. It lasted from 11 p.m. New Year's Eve until dusk the next day" (Plaisted).

The next day, the afternoon football game was to be played at Almendares Park. By all accounts it was a very physical game. "They had two ambulances and the police patrol standing on the side lines" (Oshihiyi). Besides Stetson's inability to match the Cubans physicality, the team's pre-dawn fun probably didn't do the team any favors as well. The Cuban Athletic Club shutout the Hatters 6-0. Allen coached the Stetson Hatters for another two more seasons to a 7-11 record before being replaced.

The 1919-20 Stetson Hatters football team.

The football game was played in the recently built Almendares Park (the second one), not to be confused with the original Almendares Park that was torn down. The old stadium, constructed in a fin de siècle design, was antiquated and sat only a small amount of people for ball games. The owner built the newer stadium several couple of blocks away and decided to keep the name for nostalgic purposes. For a mere 5 cents fans could hop on the city's vast network of electric trolley cars (streetcars) and it would take them to the stadium. Unfortunately, the newer Almendares Park would be completely destroyed less than a decade later by a massive hurricane. Today, the Viazul Bus Station sits on the site.

12/31/1921

The *St. Petersburg Times* headline read,

FAST CUBAN FOOTBALL TEAM DEFEATS MISSISSIPPI 13 TO 0

Squad From States Was Outclassed and Out-generaled At Every Point of Game By Fast Havana Eleven

The University of Mississippi in its first ever bowl game faced a tough challenge against the Cuban Athletic Club on New Year's Eve in Havana, Cuba. The two teams had completely different styles of playing. The CAC played by the old rules while R. L. Sullivan's Ole Miss team played the modern version. "Mississippi, failed miserably in aerial tactics, trying 12 forward passes without success" (Fast). In the end the CAC shut out the Mississippi Flood (the nickname for the team before being renamed the Rebels) 13-0 for the win but they may have received additional help from the officials. After the game Mississippi quarterback Calvin Barbour said that the Cuban squad received a number of preferential calls from the referees throughout the game. "We [Ole Miss] scored three touchdowns but they [officials] didn't let them count.

The 1921 Ole Miss Football Team

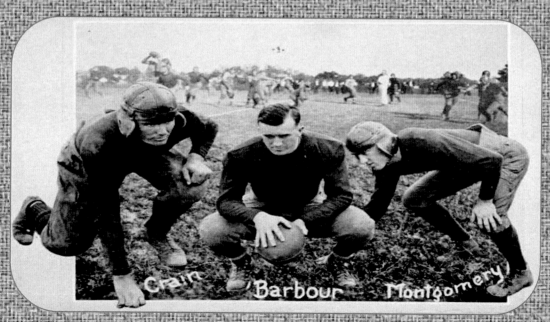

Crain   Barbour   Montgomery

We were always offside, holding or something" (Mayfield). With unbiased officiating, the football game may have had a different result. As for Coach Sullivan, the loss was his last game as the Ole Miss football coach. He did have better success with the Ole Miss basketball team as he comprised a 66–32 record as the head basketball coach.

1/10/1923

This day featured an exhibition football game between the American Legion of Tampa "Warriors" and the Cuban Athletic Club in Havana. In what was supposed to be a friendly exhibition game between the two social clubs quickly turned violent according to the Legionnaire players. "Flashing of guns by the Cuban umpire and referee, threats on the lives of the Americans if they won the game, personal physical assaults on the players, unfair and persistent penalizing and a demonstration after the game that nearly led to a clash among the spectators" (Tampa). The CAC ultimately won the game 13 to 0 but if the reports are true then the American players must have been happier just to escape with their lives. Interestingly, two years later the warriors played once again in Cuba but this time it was against the University of Havana.

The 1926 season was the University of Miami's inaugural college football season as the school itself was established just a year prior. Just a month away from the start of the

season head coach Howard "Cub" Buck (left) began looking for players to fill up his new roster. "More than 50 candidates are expected to respond judging from enrollment at the university" (Buck). As the season approached South Florida was hit by a massive hurricane that leveled the area and killed over a hundred people. The far-reaching 1926 hurricane was one of the most destructive storms to ever hit the U.S. The University of Miami scrapped plans to build a 50,000 seat on-campus stadium, opting for a smaller University Stadium to be built on the site instead. A month after the deadly hurricane struck, Miami's freshmen eleven played their first game. From then on the team was known as the "Hurricanes".

The University of Miami (white jerseys) vs the University of Havana (dark jerseys), Thanksgiving Day 1926.

Miami beat the University of Havana twice that season. They won on Christmas Day at home and on Thanksgiving in Havana. In both games the score was the same 23-0. The Hurricanes finished the season with an unprecedented undefeated record in their first season.

In the Miami Hurricanes 1928 season opener they faced the Vedado Tennis Club at home. Though the Cuban team was the heavier team, Miami had its way with islanders from the very start. "The Hurricanes rolled up 21 points before the first quarter had passes into ancient history" (Hurricanes). As the game became out of reach things got testy between the two clubs. A player Vedado player claimed that his finger was bitten during a play and the Hurricanes tackle Giebel was ejected for throwing a punch at the opponent. The University News, the University of Miami student newspaper, said that the referees made the matters worse by delaying to blow the whistle to stop action after the plays were over. When the 3rd quarter began Coach Buck put in his reserves in the game but the team continued to score at ease. "The Miami aerial attack was working smoothly and almost everyone was tossing them" (Hurricanes). In an embarrassing display of unsportsmanlike conduct, the Vedado football players were seen dancing between plays (Hurricanes). The only thing that the Vedado squad was able to do well was Rhumba, as far as the football game they were demolished to the tune of 62-0. The game proved so devastating for the club that it would be last time *Los Marqueses* football team played an American opponent.

While the game itself wasn't historically significant, the events leading up to it were. A coach and six players from the Vedado team made the 90-mile trip by airplane. "This is the first time that a foreign football team has been transported in the United States by airplane" (Hurricanes). The rest of the team were less fortunate as they caught a ferry to Key West and traveled by train the rest of the way. At that time, it costed $6 to take a ferry from Cuba to Key West while by plane it was a pricier $36.

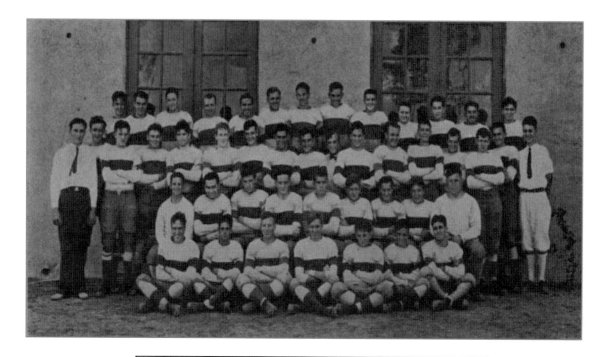

The 1928 Miami Hurricanes football team.

11/29/1929

After a near disastrous ending with Cuban authorities following the 1912 game in Havana, the University of Florida decided to play the Cubans again with the condition that the game would be played in the U.S. This time the Gators played a different Cuban

team, they played the University of Havana in St. Petersburg, Florida. The Caribes, who were coached by James Kendrigan, were heavily favored to win the game. Of the 27 members of the Caribes team that made the trip, half were chosen to their country's national all-star team. Also, the team featured a star halfback named Conrado Rodriguez who was described as the "Jim Thorpe of Cuban Football" (Future). Rodriguez held the collegiate record in the 100-meter and 200-meter dash as well as the Cuban record for the running broad jump. Charlie Bachman, the Florida head coach, sent second year assistant Nash Higgins (pictured above) and the Florida Gators reserves team to play Havana. Higgins was the varsity line coach and track head coach.

The game was to be played at a neutral site but it more like a homecoming game for the Caribes because of the large Cuban population in nearby Tampa. The day prior to the game, the Havana team were guests of the Cuban Club of Tampa. The event was a night of dinner and dancing. The buzz wasn't just centered around Cigar City (Tampa); tickets were requested as far as Key West. More bleachers were added to the St. Petersburg High School field to accommodate the sold-out crowd. Also, Cuban President Gerardo Machado and Governor of Florida Doyle Carlton were invited to attend. It's unclear if they were able to make it to the game.

In what must have felt like a David and Goliath showdown leading up to the game, the game didn't necessarily live up to the hype. The defensive units controlled most of the game and didn't allow for both offenses to get settled in. The Omelets or the Baby Gators as the Gator Reserves were commonly called beat the Caribes football team 9-0.

The Omelets

In 1933, Bachman left the Florida job to accept the same position at Michigan State College (Michigan State University). Higgins was expected to be hired as the new head coach but the athletics director opted to give the job to a younger Gator assistant in Dutch Stanley. Higgins turned in his resignation and soon thereafter accepted a unique position to be the head football coach and athletics director at the University of Tampa.

Rollins College Tars were scheduled to play the Cuban Navy but an aviation disaster scrapped those plans. On a rainy day on December 29, 1937, three Cuban Navy pilots each crashed their Stinson single engine planes minutes after takeoff, they were killed instantly. They were part of a civilian goodwill Pan American squadron that were planning to visit every country in South America. Still reeling from the loss, the navy officials decided not to play the game. Jack McDowell's Tars team was already in Cuba so he decided to split the squad in two and play an exhibition football game. With a large crowd watching at Campo Polar Stadium, the teams finished in a 26-26 tie. Despite not playing the navy team, the Tars still had plenty of fun. Coach McDowell said, "The [Cuban] Navy placed seven automobiles and drivers at the squad's disposal and showed them practically everything on the island…Cold beer out of the keg was served on the field after the game" (Gregory).

Jack McDowell must have thoroughly enjoyed his time in Cuba. In the Fall 1944, he took a 3-month leave of absence from his director of physical education position at Rollins College so that he could act as an advisory football coach for the University of Havana Caribes.

For the fifth game of the season the University of Alabama's "B" team hosted the University of Havana at home. The B team was the school's junior varsity football team. To promote the game, the local *Dothan Eagle* ran an ad on September 22, 1946 that read,

The Baby Tide or Bees as they were commonly called were led by first year freshman head coach Joe Kilgrow, a former Alabama first-team All-American halfback. Baby Tide quarterbacks Bob Cochran and Doyle Kizzire took turns running the ball down the length of the field. Kizzire scored the game's first touchdown with a 4-yard run. Alabama was able to score practically at will. "The Baby Tide rolled up 32 points in the first half for a commanding lead" (Alabama). Havana finally got on the scoreboard in the third quarter with a rare triple reserve that resulted in a 14-yard scamper for a touchdown. By the final quarter Alabama was playing with their third stringers (Alabama). In the end Alabama proved to be too strong for the Havana as they won convincingly 53-18. The player of the game honors went to Alabama left halfback John Wade who scored three touchdowns in the contest. The B team finished the season undefeated and Coach Kilegrow continued to coach the team for another 10 years.

12/7/1946

For the last game of the season the Mississippi Southern College (MSC) Southerners, who would later be renamed to the University of Southern Mississippi Golden Eagles, played the University of Havana at La Tropical Stadium in Havana. The game was called the "Tobacco Bowl" for the country's famed export and the winner of the game will be awarded a "$300 silver loving cup" (Bennett). It was the Southerners first ever bowl game appearance and the team's first full season after a 3-year hiatus because of World War II.

The 1928 Mississippi Southern Southerners

School officials on both sides feared that the game might turn into a grudge match but the teams ultimately played a clean game. "Paced by halfbacks Buster Mullin and James 'Ding Dong' Bell, each of whom scored twice, the Southerners tallied eight touchdowns" (Bennett). Coach Reed Green's Southerners would dominate the game to a lopsided 55-0 victory. Two months later, the Havana's basketball team travelled to Hattiesburg, Mississippi to play Southerners in an exhibition game. During pre-game ceremonies, University of Havana's athletics director James Kendrigan presented the Tobacco Bowl cup to the MSC school president Joseph Anderson Cook (Bennett). "Kendrigan said that Southern would be expected to defend the cup against a selected opponent the following year" (Bennett). Unfortunately, future games never materialized and Mississippi Southern held possession of the trophy. As far as the basketball game, the Caribes were able to get some payback by beating the Southerners 62-55.

11/30/1956

The 1956 football season ended with a game that was called the Annual Conch Bowl Football Charity Classic or simply the "Conch Bowl". The game pitted the Stetson University Hatters versus the University of Havana Caribes in Key West, Florida. The Lions Club of Key West organized the event and the proceeds were given to local needy organizations. Football fans were able to soak in the pre-game festivities that included a parade. During halftime there was a show that featured the Navy fleet sonar school band and drill team and Key West high school's band (Hatters).

The Stetson Hatters, led by coach Herbert "Hub" McQuillian, were anything but charitable that day. Stetson defender Terry Hollingsworth had an MVP type performance with two interceptions for touchdowns (Stetson). The Hatters dominated the Caribes 64-0 in what was McQuillian's final game. After over a quarter century of coaching, Hub decided that the 1956 season will be his last.

The actual game program.

The Stetson football coaching staff. From left to right: Assistant coach Garland Williams, assistant coach Earl Looman, head coach Herbert "Hub" McQuillian, and assistant coach Buddy Asher.

The Stetson football team was in for a bigger shock once they arrived home. The university decided to eliminate the football program entirely, which had been playing football since 1901, due to budgetary reasons. It would take over 50 years but the Stetson Hatters football program would be eventually reinstated. The 1956 Stetson-Havana game was also an important game in Cuba's sports history. The game marked the last time that any Cuban team played an American opponent in football. Shortly thereafter, there was a change in the leadership of Cuba's government. Fidel Castro's new communist regime abolished American football from ever being played on the island again.

CHAPTER NINE

Wouldn't Call It a Pipeline

Historically, the Cubans have had modest success turning their playing of football into careers. The 1940 film *Too Many Girls* summed up it perfectly. Desi Arnaz, a Cuban-born actor, played Argentine football player Manuelito Lynch in the film. Lynch was described as "the best football player in Latin America". It would have been too unbelievable for Lynch's character to be Cuban. Instead, the screenplay called for a Lynch to be from Argentina, a country that has produced roughly the same amount of professional football players. The fact is that America didn't associate the islanders with 4the sport. The one's that did go on to play did little to shift the perception. There were a lucky few that would go on to make careers of the sport.

Lou Molinet

LOU MOLINET

Ignacio "Lou" Molinet was born on November 30, 1904 in the Chaparra section of the Cuban Province of Oriente. Molinet's parents sent him to study at the Peddie School, an all-boys college preparatory school in New Jersey (Hispanic). He excelled academically and played several sports at the school. Molinet then attended Cornell University. He had become familiar with the school as his older brother was also attending Cornell. "Molly", as he was affectionately known, played football for the Big Red football. The 5'11' 195 lb. fullback had his first game action against Columbia University. It was the 5th game of the 1925 season. The Cornell Yearbook *The Cornellian* said, "Molinet, the big Cuban Sophomore, played his first game for the Varsity, and was easily the star of the game. He added a much needed punch to the backfield, and his knife like thrusts at the Columbia line were the direct cause of both touchdowns" (The Cornellian). During the football offseason he forward on the basketball team. The following football season came around and Molinet became a force on the young squad. The Cuban had dominant performances against Michigan State and Ivy League rival Dartmouth. The Big Red entered the last game of the season with a 6-1 record. Molinet scored Cornell's lone touchdown against the University of Pennsylvania. The game finished a 10-10 tie. Shortly after the season, Molinet's parents had fallen sick and he returned to Cuba to be with them. They abruptly passed away, Monliet was too distraught to return to the U.S. A telegram from the Frankford Yellow Jackets arrived for him. It was a contract to play football for the team (Hispanic). The Yellow Jackets, who would be later renamed the Philadelphia Eagles, won the NFL championship just the year before. Unable to miss this opportunity, he signed with the team and was paid $100 a game. Monliet played in 9 of the team's 17 games (Hispanic). After the season he left the team to return to his mechanical engineering studies at Cornell. He would go on to earn a membership into Cornell's prestigious Sphinx Head Senior Society which is the "highest non-scholastic honor" for undergraduates.

Molinet's single 1927 season with Frankford was marginal. It consisted of less than 100 yards total rushing and a touchdown score. Nevertheless, his play was historical. The guy who was known as "Lou" because the press couldn't pronounce his actual first name, was the first Hispanic to ever play in the NFL. He was the pioneer for future Hispanic football players to play in the league.

MANUEL RIVERO

Rivero was born in Havana, Cuba on November 3, 1908 and arrived to the U.S. at the age of 8. He was raised in the Hell's Kitchen neighborhood of Manhattan in New York City. Rivero attended Textile High School and played football for the school for two years. His play earned him an athletic scholarship to attend Columbia University. At Columbia, he lettered in football and baseball. Rivero, who wasn't the biggest football player at 160 lbs., was Columbia's starting halfback under longtime Lions head coach Luigi "Lou Little" Piccolo from 1930-33. Rivero earned captain honors and he led the team to some of the most successful seasons in Columbia football history including an unofficial Columbia national championship in 1933. After graduation, he took an assistant coaching position at the school to coach the running backs. He also had a short stint playing professional baseball from the Cuban Stars of the Negro leagues.

Rivero in a three-point stance.

In 1934, Manuel Rivero accepted a position at Lincoln University in Pennsylvania to coach all of the school's sports teams. He coached the football, baseball, track, tennis and basketball. Rivero eventually would also go on to be the school's athletic director. After 55 years at the school and 43 years coaching in various capacities, Rivero retired in 1977. The longtime head coach and athletics administrator built a lasting legacy in academia and the community. He was inducted in the National Association of Collegiate Directors of Athletics (NACDA), he received the Lincoln Alumni Association Award, and Lincoln University renamed its gymnasium the "Manuel Rivero Hall" in his honor. Rivero also served as the director of Peace Corps programs in Puerto Rico from 1963-65.

OG Joe Lamas
42 Wash Redskins
42-45 US Army

JOE LAMAS

Joseph Francis Lamas was an offensive lineman who played for the 1942 Pittsburgh Steelers. He was born on January 10, 1916 in Havana, Cuba and was sent to study at a Textile High School, a vocational school in New York. Lamas then attended Mount St. Mary's University in Maryland and also played on the Mountaineers football team. The 5'10" 216-pound guard wasn't drafted coming out of college but did sign with the Washington Redskins as an undrafted free agent. His stay with the Redskins was short lived as he was traded to the Pittsburgh Steelers on September 9, 1942 after several weeks of working out with the team in the west coast.

Lamas went on to play 8 games for The Black and Gold with the highlight being a 29-yard fumble recovery return for a touchdown against the Detroit Lions (Joe Lamas). The Steelers beat the Lions 35-7. Pittsburgh finished the season with a 7-4 record, good for 2nd place in the NFL East. More importantly, it was the Steelers' first winning record in the organization's 10-year history. Lamas received an honorable mention in the NFL's All-National League team for his play. Despite his short success in football, Lamas felt that it was his patriotic duty to serve in the U.S. military. At the time, America was fighting in World War II and like many young men he decided to join the army. The 1942 season with the Pittsburgh Steelers remained his only season of playing in the NFL.

The former football player and military veteran went on to teach high school at Iona Preparatory in New York before finally retiring in 1979. Lamas coached the school's football and baseball teams before becoming the athletics director. Lamas was posthumously inducted into the Catholic High School Athletic Association Hall of Fame. Also, the Catholic High School Football League (CHSFL) renamed the league's trophy the "Joe Lamas Memorial Trophy" in his honor. Lamas led Iona to the first CHSFL football championship in 1954.

CARLOS ALVAREZ

Born in Cuba's capital on April 1, 1950, Alvarez was 10 years old when his family fled communist Cuba. Though he didn't know much English, moving to Latin-centric Miami made the transition a lot easier. The kids in his neighborhood played football. While the sport was completely new to him, he picked it up pretty quickly. Alvarez attended North Miami High School and played football for the Pioneers. By his senior year, Alvarez had become the star running back on the team and was named to the Miami Herald's All City Team. He decided to accept a scholarship to play for the University of Florida. The "Cuban Comet", as he was affectionately called, was asked to play receiver to utilize his blazing speed. Alvarez didn't play his first season but used to time to learn about his new position. By his sophomore season he was nominated as a first-team All-Southeastern Conference (SEC) selection and received All-American honors as well.

The Cuban Comet cemented his career at Florida as one of the Gator's all-time great wide receivers. "Alvarez played three seasons (1969-71) for the University of Florida, making 172 receptions, totaling 2,563 receiving yards and scoring 19 touchdowns, all records at the time. His total yardage still stands as the most all-time for a Gator, with close to 200 yards separating him from second place" (Carlos). In 1972, Alvarez was drafted by the Dallas Cowboys in the 15th round, 390th pick overall.

Unfortunately, knee injuries that he suffered in college derailed his professional career before it began. The Comet furthered his education by graduating from the Duke University School of Law. Today, he practices environmental law in Tallahassee, Florida. Alvarez was inducted into the University of Florida Athletic Hall of Fame in 1986 and in the College Hall of Fame in 2011.

RALPH ORTEGA

Ralph Ortega (making a tackle on the left) was born on July 6, 1953 in Havana, Cuba and moved to the U.S. at an early age. Ortega attended Coral Gables High School in Miami and played on the Cavaliers football team under legendary head coach Nick Kotys and also was a shot putter. The Coral Gables team won back to back national championships in 1967 and 1968, a rare feat for a high school football team. Ortega went on to attend the University of Florida where he was a linebacker from 1971-1974. As a three-year starter, Ortega was a consensus first-team All-SEC defender in his junior and senior years. In his final year with the Gators, he was named as one of the team captains.

Ortega finished his collegiate career with 357 tackles, 12 forced fumbles, and 5 interceptions. Ortega was drafted by the Atlanta Falcons in the 2nd round (29th pick overall) of the 1975 NFL draft. His play earned him a starting linebacker position but his play slipped and he was eventually demoted to the special teams. In 1979, he was traded to the Miami Dolphins for the 3rd round pick. Ortega failed to make an impact with Miami and lasted for only two seasons. The following year was his last season playing in the NFL. During his six NFL seasons, Ortega played in eighty-one regular season games, intercepted five passes and recovered seven fumbles (Ralph).

After the NFL, Ralph Ortega became an assistant football coach at Gulliver Preparatory School in Miami and had a chance to coach his son Buck. The younger Ortega went on to play for the Miami Hurricanes and the New Orleans Saints. Ralph is best known for his tie playing with the Florida Gators. He was inducted into the University of Florida Athletic Hall of Fame as a "Gator Great". Additionally, the Southeastern Conference named Ortega an SEC Legend in 2007. Currently, Ralph Ortega works as a stockbroker in Miami.

CARDINALS

LUIS SHARPE

LUIS SHARPE

Sharpe had the longest professional career of all the Cuban-born football players but he became more known for his legal troubles following his football career. Born on June 16, 1960 in Havana, Sharpe was 6-years-old when his family fled Cuba and relocated to gritty Detroit, Michigan. Sharpe attended UCLA on a football scholarship (he didn't graduate). The 6'5" 280 lb. offensive tackle received All-American honors in his senior season was selected 16th overall by the St. Louis Cardinals (renamed Arizona) in the 1982 NFL Draft. He played 13 seasons with the Cardinals and earned three trips to the Pro Bowl. In 1994, an ACL injury forced Sharpe to retire. Sharpe played in 189 NFL games.

Sharpe began using drugs like cocaine and marijuana shortly after getting into the league. In the 1980s drug use was rampant in the NFL with stars like Lawrence Taylor and Dexter Manley becoming the poster boys for the growing trend. Sharpe was able to keep the habit in check while playing. After retirement, he had too much time on his hands and his drug addiction became unmanageable. Around the same time, his wife asked for a divorce and things quickly spiraled from there. Sharpe was in and out of jail for mostly drug-related offenses. He was shot twice during drug runs, stayed at seedy motels, and spent tens of thousands of dollars on drugs. At one point federal authorities threatened him with deportation back to Cuba if he continued breaking the law. In 2008, he pleaded guilty to four charges of possession of drugs and drug paraphernalia.

Sharpe was sentenced to 6 years in prison. While in jail his troubles continued. He was injured in a fight and had to be taken to a hospital for medical treatment. In 2013, the former Cardinal was released from prison. After his release he completed a court-ordered drug rehabilitation and has committed himself to sobriety. Today, Luis Sharpe works as a drug advocate with the youth.

APPENDIX: GAMES & SCORES

Date	U.S. Team		Cuban Team		Stadium
11/24/1906	U.S. Navy (USS *Columbia*)	15	University of Havana	0	Almendares Park Havana, Cuba
12/25/1907	Louisiana State University (LSU)	56	University of Havana	0	Almendares Park Havana, Cuba
12/25/1908	Rollins College	6	University of Havana	0	Almendares Park Havana, Cuba
12/25/1908	Rollins College	0	Havana YMCA	0	Almendares Park Havana, Cuba
1/1/1910	Tulane University	0	Cuban Athletic Club	11	Almendares Park Havana, Cuba
1/1/1912	Mississippi A&M (Mississippi State University)	12	Cuban Athletic Club	0	Almendares Park Havana, Cuba
12/25/1912	University of Florida	27	Vedado Tennis Club	0	Almendares Park Havana, Cuba
12/28/1912	University of Florida		Cuban Athletic Club	✓	Almendares Park Havana, Cuba
12/25/1915	Southern College (Florida Southern College)	6	Cuban Athletic Club	7	Almendares Park Havana, Cuba
1/1/1916	Southern College (Florida Southern College)	47	Cuban Athletic Club	0	Plant Field Tampa, FL
1/1/1920	Stetson University	0	Cuban Athletic Club	6	Almendares Park Havana, Cuba

12/31/1921	University of Mississippi (Ole Miss)	0	Cuban Athletic Club	13	Almendares Park Havana, Cuba
1/1/1923	Rollins College	80	University of Havana	0	Tinker Field Orlando, FL
1/10/1923	American Legion of Tampa "Warriors"	0	Cuban Athletic Club	13	Almendares Park Havana, Cuba
12/23/1923	Rollins College	59	Havana Police	0	Almendares Park Havana, Cuba
12/25/1923	Rollins College	45	University of Havana	0	Almendares Park Havana, Cuba
12/30/1923	Rollins College	31	Cuban Athletic Club	0	Almendares Park Havana, Cuba
11/29/1924	Southern College (Florida Southern College)	32	University of Havana	7	Adair Field Lakeland, FL
12/6/1924	Southern College (Florida Southern College)	0	University of Havana	0	Plant Field Tampa, FL
1/1/1925	Tampa AC	13	University of Havana	6	Almendares Park Havana, Cuba
1926	U.S. Marines of Key West "Leathernecks"	13	University of Havana	12	High school field Key West, FL
11/25/1926	University of Miami (FL)	23	University of Havana	0	University Stadium Coral Gables, FL
12/24/1926	University of Miami (FL)	23	University of Havana	0	Almendares Park Havana, Cuba
11/28/1927	Howard College (Samford University)	20	University of Havana	6	Almendares Park Havana, Cuba

1928	Hollywood	0	University of Havana	6	Unknown
1928	U.S. Marines of Key West "Leathernecks"	0	University of Havana	12	Unknown
10/27/1928	University of Miami (FL)	62	Vedado Tennis Club	0	University Stadium Coral Gables, FL
11/29/1929	University of Florida	9	University of Havana	0	High school field St. Petersburg, FL
12/6/1929	Georgia Military Academy	31	Cuban Athletic Club	6	Barron Park Atlanta, GA
12/15/1934	University of Tampa	38	Cuban Athletic Club	13	Plant Field Tampa, FL
12/30/1934	University of Tampa	25	Cuban Athletic Club	0	La Tropical Havana, Cuba
11/11/1938	Rollins College	7	University of Havana	6	Tinker Field Orlando, FL
11/18/1938	University of Tampa	33	University of Havana	0	Phillips Field Tampa, FL
10/11/1939	Georgia Teachers College (Georgia Southern University)	14	University of Havana	0	Womack Field Statesboro, GA
10/27/1939	Rollins College	25	University of Havana	0	Tinker Field Orlando, FL
11/17/1939	Rollins College	27	University of Havana	13	La Tropical Havana, Cuba
12/9/1939	Georgia Teachers College (Georgia Southern University)	27	University of Havana	7	La Tropical Havana, Cuba

12/23/1939	Rollins College	71	University of Havana	0	La Tropical Havana, Cuba
12/30/1939	University of Tampa	28	University of Havana	6	La Tropical Havana, Cuba
11/1944	U.S. Airforce "Flying Yanks"	7	University of Havana	7	La Tropical Havana, Cuba
11/21/1944	Miami Naval Training Center "Tars"	30	University of Havana	13	Orange Bowl Miami, FL
11/26/1944	Chatham Field "Flyers"	25	University of Havana	7	High school field Savannah, GA
12/2/1944	Presbyterian College	34	University of Havana	0	Duncan Park Spartanburg, SC
12/1945	Fort Pierce Amphibious Station "Commandos"	20	University of Havana	55	La Tropical Havana, Cuba
10/26/1946	Norman Junior College (GA)	24	University of Havana	0	High school field Norman Park, GA
11/9/1946	University of Alabama "B" Team	53	University of Havana	18	Wiregrass Memorial Stadium Dothan, AL
12/7/1946	Mississippi Southern College (University of Mississippi Southern)	55	University of Havana	0	La Tropical Havana, Cuba
11/11/1950	Jacksonville Naval Station "Fliers"	32	University of Havana	6	La Tropical Havana, Cuba
11/30/1956*	Stetson University	64	University of Havana	0	High school field Key West, FL

Date	Mexican Team		Cuban Team	
1948	National Autonomous University of Mexico (UNAM) Pumas	42	University of Havana	7
1948	National Autonomous University of Mexico (UNAM) Pumas	49	University of Havana	19
1949	National Autonomous University of Mexico (UNAM) Pumas	28	University of Havana	12
1950	National Autonomous University of Mexico (UNAM) Pumas	58	University of Havana	26
1954	National Autonomous University of Mexico (UNAM) Pumas	68	University of Havana	8

Key

✓ winner by forfeiture

*Annual Conch Bowl Football Charity Classic

**"Bacardi Bowl" (unofficial nickname)

***Original game versus Cuban Navy was cancelled, Rollins played an intrasquad game.

The 1st Almandares Park (1881–1916)
The 2nd Almandares Park (1918–1927)
La Tropical stadium (1929–present)

Date	U.S. Team		U.S. Team		Stadium
1/1/1937**	Alabama Polytechnic Institute (Auburn University)	7	Villanova University	7	La Tropical Havana, Cuba
1/2/1938***	Rollins College	26	Rollins College	26	Campo Polar Havana, Cuba
12/27/1939	Rollins College	26	University of Tampa	13	La Tropical Havana, Cuba

PHOTO CREDITS

No. 1, Football Game (Front Cover): Courtesy of the Library of Congress

No. 2, Cuban Tourism Brochure, Courtesy of the Cuban National Tourist Commission

No. 3, Vedado Tennis Club: Courtesy of the Cuban Heritage Collection, University of Miami Libraries, Coral Gables, Florida

No. 4, Pablo de la Torriente Brau: Courtesy of Creative Commons

No. 5, Army-Navy Game: Courtesy of the Library of Congress

No. 6, James H. Kendrigan: Courtesy of the Chicago Tribune; Cuban Embassy (background): Courtesy of the Library of Congress

No. 7, Keewatin Academy: Courtesy of The Milwaukee Sentinel

No. 8, Mario G. Menocal: Courtesy of the Library of Congress

No. 9, LSU-Havana Game: Courtesy of WDAM

No. 10, University Stadium: Courtesy of the Cuban Heritage Collection, University of Miami Libraries, Coral Gables, Florida

No. 11, Robert Zuppke: Courtesy of the Outing Publishing Company

No. 12, James H. Kendrigan: Courtesy of the Chicago Tribune; Keewatin Academy (background): Courtesy of the Chicago Tribune

No. 13, Football Game: Courtesy of the Library of Congress

No. 14, Havana Football Players: The Spartanburg Herald

No. 15, Football Helmet: Courtesy of the Gerald R. Ford Presidential Museum

No. 16, University of Havana patch: Courtesy of Havana Collectibles

No. 17, University of Havana building: Courtesy of Havana Collectibles

No. 18, Miguel Mariano Gómez: Courtesy of Creative Commons

No. 19, Luigi "Lou Little" Piccolo: Courtesy of the Library of Congress

No. 20, Fulgencio Batista: Courtesy of the Library of Congress

No. 21, Institute of Havana pin: Courtesy of Havana Collectibles

No. 22, Institute of Havana patch: Courtesy of Havana Collectibles

No. 23, T Formation: Courtesy of the University of Michigan Library

No. 24, Sloppy Joe's: Courtesy of Havana Collectibles; Palm Trees (background): Courtesy of the Library of Congress

No. 25, Harvey Harman: Courtesy of Auburn University Libraries Special Collection & Archives

No. 26, Clipper Smith and Jack Meager: Courtesy of Auburn University Libraries Special Collection & Archives

No. 27, Cuban President José Miguel Gómez, Harvey Harman, and Carlos L. Henriquez Jr.: Courtesy of Auburn University Libraries Special Collection & Archives

No. 28, Clipper Smith and Carlos L. Henriquez Jr.: Courtesy of Auburn University Libraries Special Collection & Archives

No. 29, The Captains: Courtesy of Auburn University Libraries Special Collection & Archives

No. 30, Wildcats on Offense: Courtesy of Auburn University Libraries Special Collection & Archives

No. 31, Game Action: Courtesy of Auburn University Libraries Special Collection & Archives

No. 32, An Auburn Defender: Courtesy of Auburn University Libraries Special Collection & Archives

No. 33, Testing Football Helmet, 1912: Courtesy of Rare Historical Photos

No. 34, Fidel Castro: Courtesy of the Library of Congress

No. 35, University of Havana pin: Courtesy of Havana Collectibles

No. 36, The Vedado Tennis Club: Courtesy of Google Images
Football Field: Courtesy of Wikimedia

No. 37, U.S. President Barack Obama with Cuban President Raul Castro: Courtesy of U.S. Department of State

No. 38, Les Miles: Courtesy of Wikimedia

No. 39, Football Game: Courtesy of the Library of Congress

No. 40, LSU Football Team: Courtesy of the LSU Libraries Digital Collections

No. 41, LSU-Havana Game: Courtesy of the LSUsports

No. 42, Tulane Football Team: Courtesy of Tulane University Archives

No. 43, CAC Football: Courtesy of the University of Florida Archives

No. 44, Levy Bass: Courtesy of the Mississippi State University Libraries

No. 45, Mississippi A&M Football Team: Courtesy of the University of Florida Archives

No. 46, Vedado-Florida Football Game Program: Courtesy of the University of Florida Archives

No. 47, The Vedado Marqueses Football Team: Courtesy of the University of Florida Archives

No. 48, George E. Pyle: Courtesy of the University of Florida Archives

No. 49, Hotel Brooklyn: Courtesy of Havana Collectibles

No. 50, 1912 Stetson Hatters Football Team: Photo Courtesy of the Stetson University Library Archives

No. 51, Newspaper Clip: Courtesy of the St. Petersburg Times

No. 52, The 1921 Ole Miss football team: Courtesy of the University of Mississippi Libraries Special Collection & Archives

No. 53, Howard "Cub" Buck: Courtesy of the University of Miami Sports Media Relations Office

No. 54, University of Miami-University of Havana Football Game: Courtesy of the University Archives, University of Miami Libraries, Coral Gables, Florida

No. 55, The 1928 Miami Hurricanes football team: Courtesy of the University Archives, University of Miami Libraries, Coral Gables, Florida

No. 56, Nash Higgins: Courtesy of Wikimedia

No. 57, The Florida Omelets: Courtesy of the University of Florida Archives

No. 58, Game Advertisement: Courtesy of the *Dothan Eagle*

No. 59, The 1928 Mississippi Southern football team: Courtesy of the McCain Library and Archives, The University of Southern Mississippi

No. 60, Stetson-Havana Game Program: Photo Courtesy of the Stetson University Library Archives

No. 61, Stetson Football Coaching Staff: Photo Courtesy of the Stetson University Library Archives

No. 62, Game Action Between the Denver Broncos and the San Francisco 49ers: Courtesy of the Library of Congress

No. 63, Ignacio "Lou" Molinet: Courtesy of the Pro Football Hall of Fame

No. 64, Manuel Rivero Portrait: Courtesy of Marita Rivero and the Rivero Family

No. 65, Manuel Rivero in a Three-Point Stance: Courtesy of Marita Rivero and the Rivero Family

No. 66, Joe Lamas: Courtesy of the Washington Redskins; Forbes Field (background): Courtesy of the Library of Congress

No. 67, Carlos Alvarez: Courtesy of the University of Florida (file photo); Ben Hill Griffin Stadium (background): Courtesy of Wikimedia

No. 68, Ralph Ortega Making a Tackle: Courtesy of the Atlanta Falcons

No. 69, Ralph Ortega Portrait: Courtesy of Wikimedia

No. 70, Luis Sharpe: Courtesy of Panini America; Sun Devil Stadium (background): Courtesy of Wikimedia

REFERENCES

"Alabama Bees Whip Havana." *The Tuscaloosa News*. 12 Nov. 1946. Web. 1 Apr. 2016.

Bennett, Gregg, and John W. Cox. *Rock Solid: Southern Miss Football.* Jackson: The University Press of Mississippi, 2004. Print.

Bob "The Little Dutchman" Zuppke. The National Football Foundation and College Football Hall of Fame. Web. 10 Apr. 2016.

Brewer, Stewart. *Borders and Bridges: A History of U.S.-Latin American Relations.* Connecticut: Praeger, 2006. Print.

Brichford, Maynard. *Bob Zuppke: The Life and Football Legacy of the Illinois Coach.* Jefferson: McFarland, 2009. Print.

"Buck Expects 50 Candidates for First Miami Grid Team." *The Independent* [St. Petersburg, FL] 16 Sep. 1926. Web. 10 Apr. 2016.

"Carlos Alvarez Enshrined into College Football Hall of Fame." University Athletic Assoc., Inc. 22 July 2012. Web. 5 Apr. 2016.

Conner, Floyd. *Football's Most Wanted: The Top 10 Book of the Great Game's Outrageous Characters, Fortunate Fumbles, and Other Oddities.* Potomac Books Incorporated, 2000. Print.

Cote, Amy. *Geni.* 29 Oct. 2015. Web. 5 Apr. 2016. "Cowboys Set Regular Season Attendance Record." *Pro Football Hall of Fame.* Web. 10 Apr. 2016.

"Cuba and Olympism." *LA84 Foundation.* 1980. Web. 10 Apr. 2016.

"Cuban Team Arrives for Game at St. Pete." *Sarasota Herald* [Sarasota, FL] 28 Nov. 1929. Web. 1 Apr. 2016.

"Coached Here." *The Courier-Journal* [Louisville, KY] 17 Jan. 1947. Web. 1 Apr. 2016.

College and Private School Directory of the United States and Canada, Volume 13. Educational Bureau Publishing Company, 1922. Print.

DeSimone, Bonnie. "Cuba Once Had Qbs, Too." *Chicago Tribune.* Web. 24 Oct. 1998. *Doc Fenton.* The National Football Foundation and College Football Hall of Fame. Web. 10 Apr. 2016.

Elias, Robert. *The Empire Strikes Out: How Baseball Sold U.S. Foreign Policy and Promoted the American Way Abroad.* The New Press, 2010. Print.

Fiorina, Steve. "High Schoolers Hope to Play Ball in Cuba." *ABC News.* Web. 8 Apr. 2016.

"Football Row in Havana." *The New York Times.* 29 Dec. 1912. Web. 1 Apr. 2016.

Foreign Claims Settlement Commission of the United States. U.S. Department of Justice. 2013. Print. 10 Apr. 2016.

"Future Gators Stars Face Test Against Cuban Team." *The Independent* [St. Petersburg, FL] 21 Nov. 1929. Web. 10 Apr. 2016.

Gregory, Kenneth. "Dixie Sports Notes." *The Spartanburg Herald* [Spartanburg, SC] 18 Feb. 1938. Web. 1 Apr. 2016.

Grigg, Oliver. "Remembering Wave's Match-Up Against Havana as Cuba, U.S. Repair Relations." *The Tulane Hullabaloo* [New Orleans, LA] 26 JAN. 2015. Web. 1 Apr. 2016.

"Hatters Meet Havana in Key West." *Daytona Beach Morning Journal* [Daytona Beach, FL] 30 Nov. 1956. Web. 10 Apr. 2016.

"Havana Scene of Big Event." *Florence Times* [Florence, AL] 29 Dec. 1936. Web. 1 Apr. 2016.

Hispanic Heritage Month: Ignacio Molinet. NFL Films, 2014. Film.

"Hurricanes Beat by 62-0." *University News* [Coral Gables, FL] 30 Oct. 1928. Web. 1 Apr. 2016.

"Joe Curtis to Coach Tulane Football Men." Los Angeles Herald [Los Angeles, CA] 11 Aug. 1907. 8 Apr. 2016.

"Joe Lamas." *Pro-Football Reference.* Sports Reference, LLC. Web. 1 Apr. 2016.

Kleinpeter, Jim. "Les Miles' Excellent Cuban Adventure." *Nola: The Times-Picayune.* 20 Mar. 2016. Web. 10 Apr. 2016.

Kurtz, Paul. "Sports Stew-Served Hot." The Pittsburgh Press. 8 Apr. 1939. 8 Apr. 2016.

Mayfield, Jack. "Oxford's Olden Days: First Postseason Game for Ole Miss." *Hotty Toddy.* 1 June 2015. Web. 1 Apr. 2016.

"NFL Looking to Increase Number of Regular Season Games, Possible Play in Cuba." *NFL Trade Rumors.* 30 Oct. 2015. Web. 1 Apr. 2016.

Oshihiyi. DeLand, 1920. Web. 1 Apr. 2016.

Other Games." *The Sun* [New Brunswick, Canada] 26 Nov. 1906. Web. 1 Apr. 2016.

Pérez, Louis A., Jr. *On Becoming Cuban: Identity, Nationality, and Culture.* Chapel Hill:
    The University of North Carolina Press, 2008. Book.

Plaisted, Ed. "When the Hats Went to Havana." *The Volusian* [DeLand, FL] 12 Oct. 1995.
    Web. 1 Apr. 2016.

Plott, Bill. "Auburn One Bowl Game Up On Alabama." *The Tuscaloosa News.* 26 Dec.
    1972. Web. 1 Apr. 2016.

"Ralph Ortega." *Pro-Football Reference.* Sports Reference, LLC. Web. 1 Apr. 2016.

Rockne, Knute. "Campus Comment." *Sunday Sentinel and Milwaukee Telegram*
    [Milwaukee, WI] 1 Jan. 1928. Web. 1 Apr. 2016.

"Rollins College Downs Havana University." *The Spartanburg Herald* [Spartanburg, SC]
    2 Jan. 1923. Web. 1 Apr. 2016.

"'Select' School for Boys Under Inquiry by U.S." *Chicago Tribune* 13 Dec. 1922. Web. 1
    Apr. 2016.

"Stetson Overruns Havana in Conch Bowl Contest." *Sarasota Herald-Tribune* [Sarasota,
    FL] 1 Dec. 1956. Web. 1 Apr. 2016.

"Tampa Grid Team Badly Battered in Cuban Game." *St. Petersburg Times* [St.
    Petersburg, FL] 11 Jan. 1923. 1 Apr. 2016.

The Cornellian. New York: The Cornell Annuals, 1925. Web. 2 Apr. 2016.

Vincent, Herb. *LSU Football Vault: The History of the Fighting Tigers.* Whitman Publishing, 2008. Print.

Walsh, Christopher J. *Where Football Is King: A History of the SEC.* Lanham: Taylor Trade Publishing, 2006. Print.

Made in the USA
Las Vegas, NV
19 December 2021

38748300R00093